COMMERCIAL REAL ESTATE

COMMERCIAL REAL ESTATE

How to
BUY • BUILD
MANAGE • SELL
and
PROFIT FROM IT

Edited by Jack Corgan

TAYLOR PUBLISHING COMPANY
Dallas, Texas

Library of Congress Cataloging-in-Publication Data

Commercial real estate.

    1. Commercial buildings. 2. Office buildings.
3. Industrial buildings. 4. Real Estate business.
5. Real estate investment. I. Corgan, Jack.
HD1393.25.C65   1968   332.63′243   85-27108
ISBN 0-87833-459-9

Printed in the United States of America

CONTENTS

FOREWORD

The commercial real estate industry has changed dramatically in the last 10 years.

This book has been written by leaders in our industry. They have seen the changes, have created many of them, and are still very active in the initiation of new trends. In short, these authors are experienced, mainstream real estate professionals.

Each author has written a chapter about a specific real estate issue, which is within the author's area of personal interest and expertise.

The topics were selected, because of their overall relevance to the field of commercial real estate as a whole. In this way, the book is *Comprehensive*. The chapters are written to provide the reader with a "what's happening" view of that particular aspect of real estate. Where appropriate, financial and statistical data are included to be sure the reader is presented with enough detail to illustrate the ideas and concepts.

In order that the book have maximum value, the writing focuses on *what to achieve* rather than *how to do* a task. The authors have learned by doing, and are presenting the things they have learned through their hands-on involvement in this very personal, people-oriented industry.

The reader will notice differences in writing style and approach from chapter to chapter. This is·intentional. The personalities and personal *styles* of the authors will emerge as the book is read. These factors have contributed to the authors' success, and it is hoped that the reader will enjoy the variety and will benefit from this information.

Every effort has been made to keep the information simple and to the point. As the reader might imagine, this is a difficult task when complex subject matter is involved, such as financing, federal taxes, and commercial construction. Yet, this is the very thing that makes this book so special. It deals with the big, complex issues which are originating real estate trends.

The book is organized to be read in conventional manner from front to back. If, however, the reader is especially interested in a particular author or subject, the reader is encouraged to read the chapters in any order desired.

Henry S. Miller, Jr.

Henry Miller is chairman of the board of Henry S. Miller Company, the Southwest's largest real estate brokerage and management firm.

Jack Corgan

INTRODUCTION
MONEY, LAND, BUILDINGS, AND PEOPLE

Money, land, buildings, and people. This is a book which deals with the proven relationships between these vital elements of successful real estate ventures. Each chapter in the book deals with a particular aspect of commercial real estate development. Real estate development, then, is the transformation of land and buildings for human use — for profit.

For the most part, these elements will be discussed from a *financial* standpoint. For instance, the acquisition of land for the design of an income-producing building will be discussed from the strict vantage point of *economic value*. In some cases, a beautiful site, heavily wooded, near a grassy meadow may have great aesthetic value, but very little economic value in the market place. In others, a building may be a design award winner, but have a floor plan that is unsuitable for efficient office leasing. If the building will not lease, in the terms of this book, it is an "ugly" building! Let us be quick to add that a beautiful office or retail building in a desirable location, with a leasable floor plan, is essential to the creation of a fine property. The real issue, however, is simply a matter of working within established marketplace priorities.

Land is the basic resource. Land is to development what steel is to automobiles. In his chapter, "Real Estate in the National Economy," (page 55) Charles Wurtzebach gives an overall view of the availability and relative scarcity of this resource. Land changes dramatically when it is developed, both in appearance and economic value. Once a commercial property has been developed, it would require an unusual turn of the marketplace to justify reconversion to its original state or alteration for another type of use. While it is possible to convert a finished automobile back to raw steel, much of its inherent value is lost when the finished product is destroyed. An obvious difference is that automobiles become obsolete while the land, which underlies a commercial development, increases or decreases in value in a

1

much more complex and unpredictable manner. External changes around the site affect its value over time, and often on a grand scale.

Buildings are a part of the public domain. Once built, they have personal, sentimental value to their users as a work place, a home, or as a place to carry on the many activities of life. People say of land, "They aren't making any more of it," and that is surely true. While buildings can be demolished, often these days new ones are being built and old ones are being restored. Buildings have a way of becoming very permanent. Consider for example, "temporary classroom buildings" that become permanent once they are put in place. Recently, in a meeting with the building committee of a client, we were asked to explain why a temporary building was placed on the site. Several members, who were new to the committee, but who had been to the site a number of times, were surprised to learn that the building was considered temporary. They had always thought it was permanent!

Commercial buildings, more than residential ones, will always need conversion and upgrading in an appreciating marketplace. Commercial land, which is available for development, is often on the fringes of earlier development. When the first buildings are developed, they are often planned for the short term, even though far greater property values will occur in the future. One reason for this is that most owners and developers cannot afford to build to that ultimate potential at the time of construction, and they certainly don't want a partially filled building on their hands for years to come. These factors contribute to new development and redevelopment, and to the types of investment taking place in today's market.

These marketplace changes are the factors that give master planning, with increasing densities and utilization, so much impact. This explains why converted downtown multi-story warehouses make such great offices, apartments, or condominiums fifty years after they are built. Raymond Nasher's retail/office complex at Northwest Highway and Central Expressway in Dallas is a good example of the evolution of value. Besides being a beautiful development — particularly the site development, with its well-designed entry lobbies and retail space — it is a good example of building for increasing densities to achieve greater and higher ultimate value over time. That's the name of the game.

Skidmore, Owings and Merrill Architects (SOM) designed a remarkable project that was a theoretical add-on skyscraper. It was a marvelously-designed building which also served that future greater and higher need. The first stage was about forty stories and the second was nearly the same. There were a number of problems to work out — elevatoring, structure, air conditioning — but the entire project became a great example of searching for creative ways to maximize the return on a single piece of land over a long period of time.

Appropriately enough, land and buildings have no monetary value if there is no commercial *need* for them. Too often, developers see their projects too narrowly. They see the commodity as office space at $20/sq. ft. or $80/sq. ft., without giving adequate thought to lease sizes, access, orientation, image, etc. There was a time when you could only get a new car in one color — black. But times have changed, options have improved, and the consumer ultimately determines what the manufacturer must offer if he wants to make the sale. The same is true in commercial real estate. Jerry Fults' chapter, "Marketing Office Property" (page 75) gives a good description of the desires of the user, the ultimate consumer of the goods and services we offer.

Opportunities in real estate investment are great, but the developer's *responsibility* is just as great. "Due diligence" is a term we hear more and more often in the real estate industry. As the industry changes to include more participants, through syndications, partnerships, joint ventures, and even "real estate CDs," it is vital to understand the dynamics of the interrelationship between money, land, buildings, and people. It's important to be cautious. It's important to be right. It's also important not to be too greedy, as evidenced by over-development and the proliferation of shoddy buildings. Not only will ill-conceived development sour the market, it will also adversely affect the lives of those who live or work nearby. Anyone who takes part in the development of spaces and facilities which serve the needs of the public has an obligation to serve those needs equitably, honestly, and fairly. It boils down to ethics, intelligence, patience, perseverance, and initiative: essential values which supersede any single industry or service. As stated above, the consumer ultimately determines what the developer must offer if the developer wants to make the sale.

THE SETTING: A PLACE TO BEGIN

On the surface, the setting is the site, the tract. Land has value in the marketplace based on the market's perception of the best use for the property. Yet, the *opportunities* in real estate are based upon the ability to see an even greater and higher use.

Things, though, are never simple. Once we start with a particular site, we immediately encounter personalities. How to gain control of the site? Is the owner willing to sell? Are there multiple owners? What does the owner think the property is worth? Does he have too much in it to make a deal? John Bruemmer's chapter on strategies for thinking about and buying real estate (page 85) provides a unique perspective on this critical area of negotiation.

The idea is to add to the setting an ingredient that will increase its value. Simply buying the property can achieve this end. Time can help, too. A change in zoning, or a closing or opening of a street will add value. Development is a broad and challenging concept which often goes far beyond the original idea. For example, the Colorado River was just a bare trickle through the parched canyons of northern Nevada and Arizona. Building Hoover Dam changed everything. Just think what that started — water for millions of homes, industries, agriculture, and recreation. You might say, "That's no big deal. It's so obvious." Like Einstein's theory or Newton's apple, it always seems simple later. The application of that simple idea changed the American West.

D/FW Airport in Texas is another example. Several years ago, before D/FW airport was even an idea, an airport was developed in almost exactly the same place. It was just south of what is now D/FW Airport. It was barely a stone's throw, and was called Amon Carter Field. Basically the same idea, but not put together in the same way. It did not succeed because it was not a true venture of Dallas *and* Fort Worth.

Later, through what was apparently a much better process, D/FW Airport, as we now know it, was started. Not only did D/FW Airport succeed, it transformed the perceived opportunities to be found in North Texas in a dramatic way. Dallas and Fort Worth are in the same place they have always been, yet construction of this major airport at the right time caused corporations to think of Dallas-Fort Worth in terms of air travel *time*. Consequently, Dallas-Fort Worth has become a headquarters location for many national and international corporations and organizations. Today, the D/FW Airport terminal buildings are being continuously expanded to meet the traveling public's needs. Because of its ingenious master plan, the airport is in place, there is room to grow, and the D/FW Airport Authority is prepared for change. Former Dallas Mayor, Eric Jonsson, said, "Make no small plans." He was right.

Boston's Quincy Market is a lively, exciting place to be. James Rouse, its imaginative developer, saw the opportunity. It was not obvious that an old meat, fruit, and vegetable market and a worn-out pier (but which was within short walking distance of the financial district), could be transformed into such a special place. Sometimes what we see with our eyes offers so strong an image that we have a hard time blanking out the obvious "here and now" and concentrating on the external factors and forces which create development potential.

It is reported that the artist, Michelangelo, would go up into the mountains and search for just the right piece of marble for a new sculpture. He said that he could see the figures in the stone. He said they were in there, just waiting to be released. Late in Michelangelo's life, he became so infatuated with the figure in the stone, that he intentionally left his sculptures unfinished to create a kind of twilight zone in his work with naked figures emerging from the stone. He attempted to give these later sculptures more of a life of their own.

We suspect Michelangelo was interested in the artistic expression of *time*. When a sculpture was finished, it was complete. Yet, in an unfinished state, as seen in his later works, there was something left, something yet to happen. A state of "becoming." An open, unresolved form. In that sense, real estate is similar. Ever changing, ever evolving. Increasing in value — or decreasing. The development that springs from the setting must occur at just the right point in time, and must increase in value with the passage of time.

The setting, physically, is either a piece of land, or land and existing buildings, in some sort of urban or suburban context. Obviously, the land itself does not possess the value per se; rather, it is the *location* of the land in the context of commercial needs yet to be satisfied which offers promise for the developer. As discussed earlier, it is not the natural beauty of the land or even its configuration, slope, or orientation that creates the major component of its value. It's where it is, how big it is, and how great the commercial demand is for what it can hold.

Sometimes external factors can be a factor, like the adjacency of the Boston financial district to the Quincy Market. On the other hand, developers often have to contend with difficult locations, such as a building site at the juncture of two major highways, with no suitable access to the site. Traffic is a major consideration. When the Dallas Cowboys played at the Cotton Bowl in the '60s, there were no major highways for immediate access to the stadium. People came down the small streets from many directions. Later a new facility was built for the Cowboys in Irving, a Dallas suburb. When Texas Stadium opened, the fans realized that the old traffic problems weren't so bad after all. Texas Stadium is located at the intersection of several major highways.

On game day, traffic backs up for miles, due to the relatively small number of access points from those highways.

When the famed Galleria was built in Houston, it created a wonderful simulated urban environment. It incorporated the benefits of urban high-rises, with panoramic views and high-rise image, coupled with the multi-use benefits of shopping, restaurants, and hotels. In addition, because it was suburban, you could easily get in and out of the adjacent parking garages when coming to and from work, and at lunch time. Now, as the Galleria has attracted other development, traffic has made it as difficult to get to as a central city location, and consequently, it no longer has the easy-in/easy-out feel of a suburban project. Such consequences are often impossible to predict, but developers must wrestle with such issues in the context of *time*.

Real estate broker Michael Young once described a particular office park development and its marketplace difficulties as "being in the middle of everything and the center of nothing." He meant that the development was only on the way to other centers of attraction. Again, how can we deal with such concerns? Just being aware of such subtle implications of location and user needs is helpful. Ron Witten's chapter (page 15) will provide some answers.

LAND

Land has controls. It used to be that a person's right of ownership of property was almost absolute — including how that property was to be used. Many communities today have, however, come to realize that new commercial developments affect the adjacent "quality of life." Thus, the "public" has acquired the rights of an "individual."

A recent article in the *Wall Street Journal* described a fantastic piece of property in Florida which had once been used as an estate. Because of local pressure, it was *permanently* zoned "single-family." Its value for developers was non-existent and consequently, the potential for buyers was extremely limited. There are many such stories. The much publicized housing and commercial project on Manhattan's Upper West Side has undergone similar difficulties, and has experienced many delays. So many expensive compromises have been made that the project may never be built.

It would not be much of a surprise in the near future to see federal legislation limiting developers' and property owners' rights. The court system has already gone a long way to "protect" the public from change. Like Willy in "Death of a Salesman," there is a nostalgic part in all of us that wants the benefits from progress and change, but not the effects. Even so, often the effects are not even real, but only imagined. Recently, I asked Craig Holcomb, a good friend who serves on the Dallas City Council, why he thought some people were so concerned about high-rise buildings. Craig said he thought it had to do with a natural resistance to change and a perception of the "ideal" neighborhood as large lots, nice houses, green grass, and big old trees. In truth, that "ideal" is becoming a dinosaur which belies many of the economic realities of our urban society as we now know it.

The land is *physical,* too. Dirt and pipes. A site's value is affected by the availability of water, sewers, power, and other utilities. A particular telephone company that serves the site can affect its value — dramatically. The ability of a city to meet its long term water needs affects every property in that region. Site limitations affect the density or intensity of development. These limitations are easily identified on the site plan, and include zoning and utility restrictions such as easements and set-backs. They also include underground structures such as subways and major non-relocatable utilities, as well as soil conditions and topography. When we first began work on the American Airlines Headquarters project, the headquarters site was in an undeveloped area between Dallas and Fort Worth. Over many years, previous owners of the property had allowed utility easements to criss-cross the property in a random manner. This was largely due to the fact that, until that time, this property was outside the major development corridors, and proper concern for a developable site had not been exercised. Fortunately, the area selected for the building itself and related site improvements was not adversely affected by these existing easements. With suitable planning, and with its proximity to the D/FW Airport and other American Airlines facilities, the site proved to be ideal — in spite of the tangle of easements.

Although soil conditions can be very important when projecting the cost of development, the inherent value of a site based on its location will tend to outweigh the effect of difficult soil conditions, such as expansive clay, or even geological faults. Still, a few reminders, such as the leaning tower of Pisa, illustrate the importance of taking those soil conditions, and other engineering concerns, into account.

BUILDINGS

Although buildings generally cost more to develop than the site itself, it is the land (that has the location) that increases in value.

Our firm offices in an historic old building in Downtown Dallas. Ten years ago, a bright developer could have bought the building for a million dollars. Today, it would take 8 to 10 times that amount. It's a great-looking building, but another building of an entirely different design in the same location would have experienced a similar increase in value.

Envisioning the "right" building and associated site improvements is crucial to a venture's success. In a hot market, the "right" building will get the highest rents. In a soft market, it can be leased. This factor is not more important than locations, but in a contest with buildings in comparable location, the "right" development wins. Consequently, the "right" development is the one which most closely matches the user's needs.

If you haven't read Ries and Trout's book, *Positioning,* we urge you to go out and buy it. It's a book about segmentation of markets, and positioning a product or service within a specific market of competing products or services. According to the authors, the "right" product (building) is like the "right" salad. If the customer enters a restaurant with the intention of spending a certain amount of money for dinner, she is very willing to spend that amount of money. Whether it's a modest or extravagant establishment, she expects appropriate quality and service for her dollar. If it's a modest priced Italian restaurant and a lettuce salad is all that is expected, the lettuce should be fresh, cold, and true green. It doesn't have to have tomatoes, anchovies, or olives to make the customer happy. But, she doesn't expect to get withered lettuce, soggy tomatoes, or bad anchovies and olives. If the restaurant owner spent even more money to provide the mixed salad and it only tastes fair, he still did not deliver. The same is true of buildings, not just in providing certain types of finishes and materials, but in providing appropriate amenities throughout. The developer cannot overspend on finishes only to have insufficient air-conditioning capacity or inadequate air-conditioning controls. Nor can he spend too much money on an air conditioning system and not provide suitable finishes for leasing and image. It absolutely has to be the right building: one that the customer is willing to "buy" lease space in.

David Lind, a partner in our firm, talks about the *appropriateness* of building design. David has worked on projects as diverse as corporate headquarters and metal storage buildings for oil drilling rigs. Very different buildings with very different needs. Yet, there is an ideal building out there on that blank sheet of paper — something like Michelangelo's sculpture. David's job is to determine the design which best suits the application, and which suits the criteria for what that building should be.

Louis Kahn, a great American architect, spoke frequently about "what a building wants to be." Kahn had a certain style, but he was always striving to achieve this "ideal" building for a given project.

Although it's a public building, not a commercial one, the Dallas Museum of Art, designed by Edward L. Barnes, is a comfortable and satisfying building. Good buildings reach out and embrace their neighbors. Ed Barnes' museum reaches out to the old First United Methodist Church across the street and neither competes with nor overpowers that fine historic structure. Stand at the front door of the Museum, and look across the street toward the Church and downtown Dallas. Notice how the brick pavement in front opens up to the full width of the church. Look at the colors of the museum's brick pavers and the colors of the brick walls of the church. Now, go inside the Museum. Notice how the building is appropriately *sized* to the art. Large enough for any display, but not overwhelming. This is in contrast to I.M. Pei's East Wing of the National Gallery in Washington, D.C. It is a magnificent building. It is exquisitely detailed, but the airiness of the central space is not only wasteful but inappropriate to the building's function. Appropriateness is not only a function of land use, but of the actual structures we place upon the land.

In the mid-sixties, when American, Braniff, and Delta airlines were competing so hotly in the South, Delta was providing on-time flights and very dependable and predictable service. Braniff began to win passengers in those regulated aviation days by pampering their travelers. The pampering led to the concept of making flying an "event," complete with special wardrobes for the flight attendants, and even airplanes painted by Alexander Calder, the internationally-renowned artist. Unfortunately, management's emphasis on the "event" de-emphasized the basics. Braniff was frequently late. In hopes of rectifying the problem, Braniff installed wall clocks in the aircraft cabins and made guarantees. When the guarantees could not be met, the clocks were removed . . . quietly. We use this only as a way of emphasizing the importance of the primary concern of the customer: the desire to have the fundamental needs and demands served first.

In real estate, there are many developers who experience the same difficulties Braniff had, and for many of the same reasons. Egos of developers and architects can get in the way. It's human nature. Searching for the major issues to address ("problems" to solve) is always more tedious, more difficult, and less fun than devising some new and inventive "answer." Anyone who has

served on a building committee or participated in the design of a
project knows that people have a tendency to jump to *solutions*
well before the task is really understood.

It is important to remember who the building belongs to. When
it is an owner-user building, it belongs to the owner. A sensitive
corporate owner will focus the building's design on the needs of
both customers and employees, and that focus becomes a design
"mandate" to the architects involved.

A recent article in *Harvard Business Review* describes the architectural design process for a small industrial corporation which
built customized components for manufacturers. The company
had grown fast, because of its strong customer bias. "If you tell us
what you want, we'll build it for you." The building design that
was developed emphasized this commitment to *customizing* for
the customer. The manufacturing area, with all the customized
products in the process of being assembled, was actually the *center*
of the building with many glass walls along its perimeter to allow
employees and potential customers to see in. The corporation's
commitment to the customer's product was made apparent in the
building design, and tended to reinforce the employees' commitment to the customer. Often the production staff tends to view
their role as very special, and forgets who the customer is. The
marketing staff generally doesn't make this mistake. You have
probably seen that cartoon about the different styles of a rope swing. The customer sees a swing as a cost effective, simple swing.
The manufacturing department sees it as a complex, Tinker-Toy
looking assembly with lots of interesting joints and such.
Sometimes developers and architects experience this problem.
Whose building is it?

In building design, *innovation* is very important and should be
fostered. Experimentation for its own sake, should not. Probably,
Philip Johnson's AT&T Building in Manhattan (the "Chippen-
dale Wall Clock") proves me wrong. Generally, however, ar-
bitrary experimentation is nothing but an ego trip — for someone. We are working on a project now for a client who is interested in developing a new building type for "high-tech" office
buildings. In this case, we are drawing on our data-processing
facility design experience to shape a building and its structure
specifically to accommodate the unique requirements of the
data-processing and telecommunications market for leased — not
build-to-suit — needs. We think it's going to work. We see this as
innovation, not experimentation. Experimentation is done on the
sketch sheets, but not built! Experimentation and brain-storming
precede innovation.

PEOPLE

While the focus is on the customer in real estate, the customer is really a person. There is a tendency to jump too quickly to the set of concerns that are *facilities* type questions. How much space do you need? What bay depths? How many outlets? How much can you pay? These are important questions, but there's more.

When a project is being planned, whether private or public, attention should be given to people as *people,* not just "users." It is just a subtle difference, but there is a specific set of concerns for comfort, easy access, food service, socialization, and other basic human needs. There are those subjective needs that must also be considered. The orientation of the building and the type of work environment are just two of many concerns that can influence a project.

Rooms without windows and rooms overlooking parking garages, or massive parking lots are inhumane and self-defeating. There is nothing worse than the personal feeling that you perform a meaningless task, or work in a dead-end job. The facility the company provides as a workplace says a great deal about the individual's importance to the organization, his career potential, and his future. It really is important, and becomes a fundamental design concern.

The American Airlines Southern Reservations Office which we designed, has been called the best building of its type in the world. It is a fine building for employees because American wanted it to be that kind of building. American's reservations agents, like many of its staff, work one-on-one with American's customers, every day, around-the-clock. The importance of a positive impression over the telephone is critical. The reservations office is designed around the needs of the reservations agents from an emotional and practical perspective. It is a comfortable, convenient, and stimulating work environment. In this case, the designer and the client jointly evolved the form and function, and the result has been a gratifying success.

RESPONSIBILITY TO SOCIETY

Last summer when my wife Carol and I took our children through Carlsbad Caverns, I asked one of the Park Rangers about the extent of the caverns that had been explored and mapped. "There are many, many miles of unexplored passages," she told me. "The public is admitted to about half of the known area that has been charted. But," she said, "I doubt they will ever let the public into any more of the cave. They would just ruin it." When asked what she meant, she shined her flashlight down on the ground in the natural area, just off the path. Not far from the sign, which asked visitors to stay *on* the path, were hundreds of footprints in the moist floor of the cave. It was evident there were many visitors who had no respect for this great natural resource, nor did they particularly care whether they preserved it for future generations or not.

Even with the best of intentions, humans can be very hard on our environment. The concentration of people, and their attendant conveniences such as personal automobiles, generates air pollution in areas of large population. In some cases, entire *regions* are blighted by air pollution.

The earth has been evolving for years and years. Natural disasters, such as floods and wind erosion, can mar natural beauty. But we are not talking about disasters. We are talking about the conscious transformation of the natural environment into a developed environment for human use — frequently for profit. *"Profit is a good word,* but like other business morals, the acquisition of profit in real estate development must be consistent with the highest standards of business ethics.

The golden rule applies. Think about those people who own property adjacent to the property that you are developing. Think about those people who own no property, but who live or drive through the area in which your development will occur. If you were any one of them, would you want to meet the builder after he had completed the first phase of your development? Would you approach the developer and say, "Gosh, I'm really glad you built that development. It's such an enhancement. I love that sculpture you put out there and the way you screened the parking."

Most development is for a lifetime. You've heard that sad, worn-out expression about doctors "burying their mistakes." Real estate developments are a built expression of their makers that last for years.

A few years ago, I was interviewing a professional photographer to shoot some architectural photography for us. I had heard good things about him, and was hopeful that we could afford him. When he came into our office to negotiate the work to be done, he said, "I just have to ask you this. Did your firm do that ugly building down the street with the yellow and white panels? It's just awful, and I just can't imagine working with someone who would do something like that." Fortunately, we didn't do the building. It just points out that all people involved with a development are attached to it, for better or worse, in a strong and permanent way. If one gets to thinking about this too hard, it can easily stifle development. This is not the point. However, the responsibility is real for all developers.

The exciting thing about *responsible* development is the fact that it is imitated. As much, if not more than any other type of business, new design ideas, colors, and materials are transferred quickly. When you work hard to do good design, you not only improve the immediate area, but the transfer of ideas occurs widely across the country, and even the world, in some cases.

The proper transformation of land and buildings for human use and profit can be successfully accomplished by getting the facts, being honest with oneself, and executing the development with painstaking care. The chapters which follow will provide some "inside" facts and approaches to each aspect of commercial real estate development.

Read and profit.

Jack Corgan is a principal with Corgan Associates Architects, one of Dallas' largest design firms. Mr. Corgan has served as principal-in-charge of major architectural projects for such clients as American Airlines, IBM, and Dallas/Fort Worth International Airport.

Ronald Witten

REAL ESTATE — ANOTHER CONSUMER PRODUCT

For most of modern history, conventional wisdom has held that the three keys to successful real estate development are "location, location, and location." This approach to development strategy worked well in the 1970's and prior. Markets weren't terribly competitive; over-building generally was localized and short-lived. Developers weren't particularly creative, since they were operating in a landlord's market. And, the end users of real estate (e.g. apartment renters, office tenants, retail shoppers) had relatively few choices in which specific offices or apartments, etc. selected. In that environment, the customers were real estate neophytes — inexperienced, unsophisticated, almost naive.

Real estate in the 1980's takes on a different complexion. Huge investment flows from S&L's, syndicators, and investors into real estate have caused record levels of commercial construction — more product than most markets can use in the short term. With developers large and small pumping out new projects, the commodity in shortest supply today is *users!*

In this new environment, the key motto for development success will be "The Customer is King." This reorientation toward the market will place real estate development on the path of more mature American industries. For example, in their early days, automobiles were available from Ford Motor Company in any color you liked, as long as the color was black. Since then, greater competition has forced the automotive giants to refine their designs and build the cars customers want. Like most mature industries, the automotive business has thus become market-driven. The same transition is found in the gasoline/service station business post OPEC embargo, in computers, in banking/finance, indeed finally in telephone service.

So, the most important fundamental shift in real estate development in the 1980's will be a greater sensitivity to the end user — his specialized needs and preferences.

NEW GROUND RULES FOR DEVELOPMENT

In real estate development, the old days (and good old boys) are gone. New ways of doing business, new players, and new roles for old players have forged a new set of rules for successful real estate development. Some carry over from the old days, but others are fundamentally different.

Elements For Success

Several ingredients are critical for success in this game of real estate development. A typical development project might involve these steps:

1. Selecting a site to develop
2. Preparing preliminary product design and development economics
3. Securing financing
4. Obtaining governmental approvals
5. Finalizing product design
6. Building the project
7. Marketing the project

To be successful, then, a real estate developer must ably manage a wide range of diverse functions and people. Market analysts refer to absorption rates, supply/demand and unmet customer needs as niches in the market. Structuring acceptable financing requires enough financial knowledge and sophistication to sell his banker and financiers on the plan.

Securing the desired zoning for a piece of property demands an ability to work jointly with sometimes unrealistic city employees and with sometimes irrational homeowners groups, each with a different perspective than the developer. Once past these obstacles, the developer works arm-in-arm with another distinctly different group of individuals — the design and construction team. Here, innovative architects want to create a building that "makes a statement." Bespectacled engineers talk about stresses and loads. Ruddy-faced construction foremen worry about rain delays before they're "dried in" (building shell completed).

The successful developer then is a chameleon — multi-lingual and multi-faceted.

Once he has run the gauntlet and met all these demands, the developer is ready to attack the marketing phase. With a cadre of enthusiastic leasing or sales personnel, this new development "can't help but succeed." Right? Unfortunately, numerous developers have reached the marketing phase only to find that the project doesn't perform up to expectations. In analyzing why, each step of the process is questioned. Did the financing place too great a burden on the project? Did our zoning keep us from competing effectively? Did poor quality construction turn customers off? Was our marketing effort handled improperly? Any or all of these can be at fault.

In our experience, though, disappointing projects can be traced more often to *inadequate or misdirected product planning and design* than to any other single factor — selecting the wrong location, designing the project based on the developer's or lender's "gut feeling" rather than on customers' needs, or targeting the wrong kind of customer in design and marketing.

The balance of this chapter discusses techniques developed to help the developer avoid such land mines.

More Competitive Real Estate Markets

A Volatile Economy = More Risk.

The early 1980's marked a watershed in American business in general and in real estate development in particular. Recurring double digit inflation, unprecedented interest rates and uncertain consumer spending caused the U.S. economy to grow more volatile than any time in post-war history. Prime interest rates over 20 percent and a three-year recession from 1980 to 1982 magnified the uncertainty of the already risky real estate development business.

In response, developers began to study each step in the process more closely to find ways to minimize downside risk, hence, the growing popularity of financial hedges — interest rate futures, rate puts, arbitrage, buying future commitments. Closer study produced streamlined construction processes, which shortened construction periods and, thus, minimized interim financing costs as well as market risk. Interest also grew in more detailed product planning and design to be sure that the project would meet customers' needs once ready for occupancy. That is, these more challenging times are causing developers to grow more sophisticated, to fine tune their operating procedures and, thus, wring out any inefficiencies.

Just as important, those tough times accentuated the importance of "deep pockets." Developers who were financially strong enough to develop properties even when market demand was relatively weak outperformed those who stopped building in the down market of 1980-1982. A good example of the value of financial strength is Carl Summers, one of the country's most active apartment developers. The Summers Companies continued to build through the times of high interest and economic uncertainty, starting almost as many units in Dallas, in 1980-1982 for example, as they had in the heyday of 1977-1979. The experience, expertise and reputation gained from this on-going building program helped cement the financing sources, site availability and marketing team to enable the Summers' interests to start 1,800 apartments in Dallas-Fort Worth in 1983-1984.

Another obvious example is the Trammell Crow organization. In the face of an uncertain economy in 1980-1981 and a growing number of downtown developers, the Trammell Crow Company started San Jacinto Tower (1981) and LTV Center (1982) to bring on over 1.75 million square feet of office space in downtown Dallas. This aggressive building program strengthened the Crow organization's grip on the top spot in the downtown Dallas office fray, and added two successful and attractive buildings to Dallas' skyline.

Granted, most developers don't have the financial strength of a Carl Summers and certainly not a Trammell Crow. To get those "deep pockets," many developers have formed partnerships or joint ventures with financial institutions. Teamed with a sound insurance company or savings and loan association, the developer of the 1980's is protecting himself from the possible whipsaw effect of skyrocketing interest rates or economic recession that could spend his assets in short order.

Thus, the greater economic volatility of the early 1980's has encouraged risk sharing between developer and lender, as well as growing sophistication in running a development company.

Financial Institution Deregulation Makes New Bedfellows

At the same time that developers were scratching their heads over how to live through a tough market, lenders were greedily eyeing the profits made by developers on recently built projects for which they had provided mortgages. Led by the major life insurance companies, financial institutions pursued equity positions in new projects they would finance. Joint ventures (JV's) were formed to develop new projects (especially office buildings initially) in which developer and lender shared ownership. These insurance company joint ventures focus primarily on rather large projects and have produced such major buildings as Interfirst Plaza in Dallas.

But, these life insurance company JV's only scratched the surface in terms of volume of new projects. The real firestorm came from savings and loan associations. After the near-collapse of the thrift industry in 1980-1981, new regulations effective in 1982 allowed S&L's to participate more aggressively in real estate development. Most thrifts capitalized on this change and, seeking to diversify out of single-family mortgage lending, aggressively pursued income-property developers as JV partners.

Super Developers Mean More Projects

So, developers entered the 1980's with greater financial security. Financial institutions entered the 1980's seeking profits in development joint ventures. The result? Predictably, these Super Developers — the developers paired with a strong lender — can, and do, produce more projects than before. The developer's long-time constraint of limited financial capacity was overridden by his new financial partner. The lender's internal control mechanism — fear of bad loans — was overridden by the desire to realize profits from both fees on new loans today and future capital appreciation. That is, by pairing up, developer and lender alike lose their fears, and more projects get built than they would otherwise have under the borrower-lender roles of the past.

Syndications Fuel the Fire

On top of the Super Developers has come another massive new investment force in U.S. real estate. Syndication firms invest the capital of individual Americans, raised in increments as small as $1,000 or $5,000, in commercial real estate seeking tax shelter now and capital appreciation later. The remarkable success of firms like JMB Realty (now JMB-Federated) and Hall Financial Group in channeling the small investor's funds into real estate has created additional motivation for developers to build: "Even if the end users aren't there to fill the project, I can sell it to a syndicator at a profit."

SUCCESSFUL DEVELOPMENT IN THE 1980's

All these trends point toward the continuation of a highly competitive marketplace for users — tenants who pay rents for apartments, offices, warehouses, etc. In effect, the new techniques of funding the real estate markets can produce more product than the marketplace can absorb. So, the secret to successful development in the future should lie in capturing more than your fair share of tenants in the marketplace at attractive lease rates.

More Competitive Markets Make the Customer King

With the new ground rules for the 1980's, the real estate marketplace will remain more competitive than in the past. Most

developers have recognized that fact, and are changing their mode
of operation (M.O.'s) accordingly. Each developer is seeking a
competitive advantage over his colleagues, a means of drawing
customers to *his* office building, or apartment community or
shopping center.

For example, perhaps the most apparent tool being used to
establish this superior competitive position is *architecture*. From
distinctive downtown skyscrapers of post-modern style to art-
deco strip shopping centers to Cape Cod style apartments, the
1980's developer is creating more aesthetically interesting projects. This added attention to architectural quality has begun to
pay dividends to developers, as tasteful distinctive buildings have
been very well received in the marketplace. Tenants enjoy a more
pleasant, more prestigious environment, and the general public
benefits from a more attractive cityscape. Perhaps Gerald Hines
Interests offers the best example of architectural leadership in its
office buildings. Beginning with Pennzoil Place in Houston in the
mid-1970's, the Hines organization has consistently stressed architecture (even in strong markets!). This philosophy of offering
the *customer* a better quality environment has combined with the
other ingredients for success to establish Hines as one of the best
— as well as one of the biggest — developers in the U.S.

Architecture is only one means of drawing in the real estate user
though. And, once every developer commissions a distinctively
designed building, this competitive edge wears away. *Satisfying
the customer can't stop at the surface.*

Another means of gaining a leg-up over competitors is more effective *marketing* once the project is built: persistent, enthusiastic
leasing or sales efforts, creative advertising and promotion,
rent/price concessions. All these are means of maximizing your
market success once the project is underway or finished.

But one tool can pay even greater dividends than architecture
or marketing — prior to product design: *market research.*

The concept behind this tool is simple. Market research allows
the customer (in this case, the real estate user) to convey his needs
and preferences to the manufacturer (here, the developer). For
decades, market research has told Proctor & Gamble how to alter
or redesign or reposition its toothpaste, detergent, and deodorant
products. It helps General Motors match special products to
special market segments. By knowing *who* is buying Ivory soap
and *why,* P&G can be sure that Ivory's advertising, pricing, and
packaging are consistent with their buyer's interests.

Proctor and Gamble and General Motors have one big advantage over the real estate developer, though — the flexibility to

change design after reaching the market. Instead, the real estate developer makes decisions in the product planning and design stage that are essentially irreversible. Once an office building's footprint (ground floor plan) is set, or an apartment's unit sizes and mix are determined or a shopping center's configuration is designed, redesign is normally economically impossible. So, each real estate development reaches a point of no return. In effect, every development's eventual market success can be no greater than the quality of product planning and design that went into the process early on.

The finality of these initial design decisions and the intensified competiton for end users in most real estate markets have forced advances in the state of the art of real estate market research in the recent years. *Ten years ago,* our clients were asking questions like: How many apartments should I build at my site now? *Today,* that question is: Is there more than one renter type for my site and how many units can I build for each?

Figure 1

MARKET RESEARCH IN THE REAL ESTATE DEVELOPMENT PROCESS

Research Task	*Answer*
Economic growth, current and recent past Economic diversity Supply/demand balance in pertinent real estate product	Select metropolitan area with greatest development opportunity
Supply/demand balance by neighborhood Rental/price achievement by neighborhood	Select neighborhood with greatest development need
Success/Failure of competitive products Customer interviewing series Consumer segmentation	Design product to fit customers' needs at your site

Ten years ago: How many one-bedroom, two-bedroom and three-bedroom apartments should I have? *Now:* What floor plan types do I need to satisfy each target renter (small or large one-bedroom/den, two-bedroom single-parent plan, two-bedroom/den roommate plan, luxury efficiency)?

Then: What office rents should I aim for in my new building? *Now:* What can I expect to achieve in rents next year when my building is finished, considering premiums for floor location and view, parking charges, and rent concessions?

Then: Is there enough demand to fill a 140,000 square-foot shopping center at my location? *Now:* What mix of tenants do I need to best meet the shopping needs in my Trade Area?

The net result of these increasingly difficult questions has been the development of more sophisticated analyses in the market research process. From the studies that we have done over the years, a model approach has evolved that seems to answer the key questions at the right time:

- Selecting the right place to develop, and
- Tailoring the product design to the customer.

Figure 1 (on page 19) graphically displays this process.

Where to Develop

Although not all developers use this approach (see "Short-Circuiting the Process," page 27), these two steps can assure that project planning gets off on the right foot. The starting point is deciding which *metropolitan area* offers the best opportunity for the kind of product you want to develop (homes, warehouses, offices, apartments, etc.). In past years, most developers worked only in their hometowns, so this decision was made by default. With the evolution of the Super Developers and their financial resources, developers have grown increasingly active "out of town." Today, a developer from a major city such as Dallas, Houston, or Atlanta is almost guaranteed to run across one or more of his hometown competitors in another city's airport. As a result of this geographic flexibility, selection of which metro area or areas to pursue is of greater concern.

Two philosophies can be used in selecting the right metro area. One follows the idea of finding niches — markets whose need for commercial space or housing has not been fully satisfied. Because of its strategic nature, let's refer to this M.O. as the *fox* approach. The second approach, which we refer to as the *gorilla* approach, simply targets metro areas with good mid- to long-term growth potential, ignoring competitive market conditions today or next year. As the name implies, the second approach works best for large, strong development companies who can compete through the tough markets without suffering permanent damage. Conversely, the approach more appropriate to the mid- and small-sized developers appears to be that of the fox — finding niches of untapped opportunity.

Some of the key factors we would look for in seeking out niches and identifying an attractive Growth Market for new development are these:

- strong economic growth locally in the past year or so *and* in the past five years,
- a diversified employment base (Be careful of one-industry towns) with some high-growth industries represented,
- no obvious signs of severe overbuilding of your product type.

Given existing data sources, selecting (or at least prioritizing) the best metro area can be done solely from desk-top research, whether using the fox or the gorilla approach.

For example, an office developer client was looking for two new metropolitan areas in which to create an ongoing building program of fairly modest proportions (100,000 square feet of office space per year). The gorilla approach would have suggested that Dallas/Fort Worth and Phoenix were the places to be — rapidly growing, well diversified economies. Indeed, Dallas/Fort Worth was the country's leading area for office space absorption. Similarly, Phoenix's economic growth outstripped even Dallas', although total office demand was not as great.

Yet, a more detailed analysis at the time showed that Atlanta and Orlando both had sound economies with very respectable growth rates (although behind Dallas/Fort Worth and Phoenix) *and* also did not have the excessive competition found in Dallas/Fort Worth and Phoenix. The strategist would perhaps choose one of these markets and avoid banging heads in the gorilla markets.

Once you're in the right metropolitan area, the next logical question is — which *neighborhood* or district offers the greatest potential? Where should I look for a building site?

The gorilla/fox mentality applies to this question, too. In most metropolitan areas, one or two geographic pockets frequently dominate the metro's new building activity — the Dallas Parkway area in Dallas' office market, the Tech Center/I-25 corridor in Denver's office market, the East Valley corridor in Phoenix's apartment market, etc., etc.

Assuming that these dominant areas will remain on top for the future, the gorilla would buy a site in the heart of this hotbed of new building, regardless of how overbuilt this pocket might be this year or next. Conversely, the fox would pick out the path of least resistance — where the leasing is apt to be *least* difficult. In analyzing Austin's condominum market, for example, the gorilla's safe money would choose the Northwest Austin area — sales were steady and proven, the competition was formidable but not damaging, and the lenders all thought that was the place to be. However, closer analysis revealed an unmet need in Near South Austin. Sales nearby were strong enough that all inventory would soon be sold, and only two other small projects were in the pipeline for future construction. In this situation, research identified a shortage of supply that the gorilla would have ignored, but the fox capitalizes on.

Tailoring Your Product to the Consumer

By now, you should have selected the right metropolitan area and the right location within that metro for your product type. Don't relax — the most valuable answers still lie ahead.

Whether you've selected your site like a gorilla or like a fox (or like an ostrich, ignoring the facts), *the key to successfully drawing your customers to your project lies in offering the product they most want. Find out what your customers are looking for in your product and give it to them.* Sounds simple-minded and obvious? Yet, it is — just like most of the basic principles of doing business.

In reality, most real estate product design is based on input from the developer, the architect, the city building official and the lender. Usually, the developer is struggling to maximize the economic return on paper; the architect strives to provide an aesthetic edge over the competitors' design; the city building official wields power to enforce building ordinances and codes; and the lender too often requires that the project design fall within the standards of other projects he has financed that haven't gone bad.

Certainly, these are all valid considerations and all these sources do provide important input. The problem is that, in all likelihood, not one of these individuals — much less their consensus — closely reflects the attitudes, needs, and preferences of the project's end user. How can a successful developer relate to what's important in an apartment to a 25 year-old divorcee with one child? Or to the concerns of a Xerox sales office manager in selecting office space? Or to the shopping needs of a 32-year old husband/wife/two-child household in a new tract home neighborhood?

The point is simply that the developer of the 1980's needs a direct objective channel of input from his customers if he's to gain a *real* advantage over his competitors and reap the benefits of better meeting his customers' needs as a result.

How can a developer establish this channel of input? The keys to receiving meaningful, reliable input are *objectivity* and *methodical analysis.* Valuable input can sometimes come from the opinions of leasing/sales staff, from property managers, and from developers — but underscore the *sometimes.* These individuals are intimately familiar with their jobs and do have a great deal of knowledge. As with all human beings, however, their opinions and judgment tend to be influenced by their most recent experiences, not necessarily the entire picture. An apartment manager who has leased 20 of the last 40 units to college student roommates will tend to report college students as the project's primary resident type even if few had leased there previously. The office leasing agent who has signed four sizeable leases with high-tech companies in the past four months tends to forget the insurance agents and accounting firms he/she may have seen in the meantime. We remember the memorable.

Think back. In shopping competitors' projects, how often have you heard the agent or developer explain that they have "a good mix of tenants?" The same is true of what the tenants like about their project: "It's a good location for them and they like our amenities." Is that all there is to it? Usually not.

So, to get clear, direct input from your customers, the developer needs some anonymity (to solicit the complaints as well as the praise) and also the expertise of a market research firm to analyze the customers' needs thoroughly and methodically.

Let's be more specific. *Two processes* should be involved in defining your customers' wants. *First, the actual experience of your competitors* may turn up some do's and don'ts. Be sure not to stop there, though. By emulating the most successful project in your area, you're doomed to do no better than that project. You won't likely improve on its performance!

The *second* step is a series of *in-depth interviews with your customers.* By discussing their needs directly with them, your researcher will be able to understand what those successful competitors did right and wrong, but also, *why* and *what they could have done better.*

Contrasting two recent studies conducted for office developers facing similar projects illustrates this concept.

First, one developer came to us with a five-acre site in a suburban North Atlanta area that allowed construction of up to 120,000 square feet of office space, within a 120-foot height restriction (i.e., 10 floors). Design options thus ranged from a 10-

story building with 12,000 square-foot floors to a four-story building with 24,000 square-foot floor sizes. The economics of the two extremes appeared similar, so the key issue came down to which building would lease better — faster and/or at higher rents. That is, which building would the office users attracted to that area select? To date, the only buildings found nearby were low-rise or small mid-rise projects of four or fewer floors. One four-story building offered larger floors (22,000 square feet) and had achieved the highest rents in the market, while leasing moderately well. This project's success would perhaps sway the design choice to the four-story option. However, a thorough survey of tenants in that building and in others nearby revealed the tenants to be a mixture of small and medium sized firms who were seeking identity and prestige in their offices. They associated both these factors, of course, with the largest office building in the neighborhood: then the four-story 22,000-foot floor project. This finding clearly pointed toward the appeal of building a high-rise "landmark" building on our client's site — not the four-story design proven successful nearby.

A few years later, we received virtually the same assignment in the Dallas/Fort Worth area — a choice between mid-rise with larger floors and high-rise with small floors. In contrast to the Atlanta project, the tenant survey here revealed that, while the space users were local and regional firms (not national), their businesses were growing rapidly and they were in need of 50 percent more space than they occupied, or an average of 11,000 square feet per firm. New buildings nearby were offering 12,000 to 15,000 square-foot floors and had been leasing successfully. However, the tenant profile suggested that being able to have future expansion space on the same floor would be a valuable asset in leasing, so the study recommended the mid-rise route rather than high-rise.

Despite its benefits, one of the pitfalls of market research can be that the customer expresses interest in more space or more amenities than he can afford. So, building in checks and balances also becomes critical to a meaningful research program. Let's look at an apartment market study we were involved in recently in San Antonio. Our door-to-door survey of residents leasing newer apartments nearby showed good incomes, two wage earners in most households, no children, blue-collar occupations, and mature ages (25-39). In the survey, these residents expressed a strong interest in three-bedroom apartments (or two bedrooms plus a den). At the necessary 55 cents per square-foot rents, a three-bedroom unit of 1,200 square feet would lease for $660 per month. This translated into an income requirement of $56,000 per year (at the 14 percent of income typically spent on housing by individuals at that income level). Unfortunately, only 7 percent of the targeted renters could qualify for that rent level. As an alternate solution, though, the survey results also indicated that these residents felt they could give up space in their present living rooms and in their dining areas. By reducing those space allocations, a functional two-bedroom/den floor plan was designed in 1,075 square feet and targeted at the 25 percent of the renter groups which could afford $595 per month. In this instance, a simple read-out of the research would have recommended units that wouldn't have leased — too large for renters' budgets. Fine tuning produced a very workable floor plan that met the customers' needs and their budgets.

Consumer Segmentation — Avoiding More Pitfalls

As mentioned earlier, real estate product design is frequently determined by committee, by the seat of the pants, or by the most recent set of plans off the shelf. Market research can improve on this intuitive approach to design, but it, too, can miss the mark without attention to consumer segmentation. Let me explain what we mean. Hardly any group of customers is homogeneous. Apartment or office tenants, patio home buyers or others tend to include one or two dominant customer types and perhaps four or five miscellaneous types. Without zeroing in specifically on the needs of the customer type you want to attract, even the most comprehensive market survey won't be of any value. For instance, an office market may be composed of a) numerous small local firms, and b) a scattering of large national firms. In that instance, aiming at the "average" user would miss both market segments.

Similarly, an apartment resident survey showed an average age of 29 years and an average household income of $36,000. These facts might suggest an upwardly mobile, young professional audience, and a need for spacious, well-amenitized one and two-bedroom units. A closer look, though, clearly indicated that our client should build two completely separate apartment communities on the site rather than one — a 220-unit project of small units for the young singles comprising 45 percent of the total market, and a 160-unit luxury community for the mature professionals and early empty nesters representing 35 percent of that neighborhood's renters.

Short-circuiting the Process

The ideal market research program for real estate development starts with selecting the right metro area, followed by buying a site

Figure 2

A SHORTCUT VERSION OF
MARKET RESEARCH IN THE REAL ESTATE DEVELOPMENT PROCESS

Research Task   *Answer*

Supply/demand balance in the neighborhood near your site
Rental/price achievement in your site's neighborhood

Market feasibility of developing
in your location

Success/failure of competitive products
Customer interviewing series
Consumer segmentation

Design product to fit customers'
needs at your site

in the right neighborhood, and completed by identifying who the project's *real* customers will be and how the project should be designed to meet their needs.

That's the ideal, and some far-sighted, proactive developers do plan their efforts in that manner. In many instances, though, the development process is triggered not by planning site selection or perhaps even metro area selection, but rather by a piece of property being presented to the developer by a broker. That circumstance obviously cuts out the early part of this complete research process. The questions that remain to be answered have to do with evaluating the supply/demand balance in the area around our site and projecting the absorption potential of our proposed project. If no red flags show up there, then the research focuses on determining the product we need to provide for our customers. This shortcut approach is depicted in Figure 2.

OUTLOOK

Real estate development in the 1980's is faced with a new environment of greater risks, growing complexity, and intense competition. These forces are causing real estate to emphasize the customer and his/her needs on everything from amenities to architecture, lease concessions to floor plans. While this trend is somewhat novel in real estate, extensive research and careful preplanning are already characteristic of most major American businesses today. Just as in other industries, the needs of the customer — the end user — are shaping new real estate development plans of the 1980's.

In the future, more and more real estate developers, commercial and residential alike, will add market research to their repertoire of disciplines. The direct channel to the customer, which market research can provide, will become a critical competitive advantage for developers in the more challenging marketplace of the future.

Ron Witten is president of M/PF Research, one of the largest real estate market research firms in the United States, which analyzes real estate markets throughout the southern U.S.

Since joining M/PF in 1973, Witten has been active in all three M/PF product groups: individual market feasibility studies, published real estate market reports, and professional seminars. M/PF serves builders, developers, lenders, and investors in evaluating market opportunities for acquisition and development of housing, commercial, and mixed use properties.

Leslie Finks

INCENTIVE TO BUILD

Real estate plays a particularly significant role in American society. The livelihood and well-being of virtually every American is affected by the supply of residential and commercial real estate. Congress has recognized its importance to the economy by including numerous tax incentives in the Internal Revenue Code for real estate investments. To realize maximum benefit from these favorable policies, investors must know the pros and cons of each and then proceed with a well-planned strategy.

We will discuss certain provisions of the Internal Revenue Code affecting commercial real estate developments, and we will suggest tax planning opportunities for such investments. Also, we will discuss current trends in Congress to eliminate abusive tax shelters and increase federal revenues. These efforts may adversely affect persons who invest in real estate where there is little or no economic benefit to be realized, but persons who acquire real estate as a sound business investment should continue to realize favorable tax treatment on their investment.

UNCLE SAM, MOTHERHOOD, APPLE PIE, AND REAL ESTATE

Throughout American history, our system of government has favored the ownership and development of real estate by a broad segment of the population. Many of the early settlers migrated to this country because of the incentives that colonial governments provided for ownership and development of real estate. Throughout the nineteenth century, the United States encouraged real estate use and improvement on the frontier by making land available free or at nominal cost to frontier farmers. The government also fostered the growth of railroads to facilitate migration to the frontier. During the Great Depression, the President and Congress developed programs to assist farmers, homeowners, and businessmen in retaining their real estate holdings. Government policies have reflected the view that real estate ownership by a broad segment of the populace enhances our democratic system of government and, accordingly, government should provide incentives for private real estate ownership and development.

31

Real estate development plays a vital role in today's economy. It provides employment in construction as well as in related industries such as timber, steel, appliances and household furnishings. Development also makes residential and commercial real estate plentiful and affordable. In the inner city, real estate development is essential to prevent urban decay, poverty, and crime.

The real estate industry is vulnerable to changes in the economy. It is generally the first industry to suffer the effects of a recession and the last to recover. During depressed economic periods, unemployment in real estate construction generally averages twice the unemployment rate for other industries. While the real estate industry must compete for investment dollars, tax incentives keep real estate investment competitive with other industries. Simultaneously, the incentives help maintain the level of capital required for future development.

Real estate constituencies have had a significant impact on legislation through strong representation in Congress. Groups representing real estate agents, home builders, commercial developers, labor unions, and syndicators frequently join together to express their needs. They have also protested loudly the efforts of those who would alter the status of the industry in the American system.

Tax Incentives

The tax incentives provided by Congress benefit developers and investors by permitting them to defer income recognition, convert ordinary income into capital gain, and reduce tax through investment credits. Careful tax planning with a tax advisor is required to capitalize on all these benefits.

In order to incorporate tax planning concepts into business operations, the investor needs to become familiar with basic tax law concepts affecting real estate. The following paragraphs summarize certain provisions dealing with the Accelerated Cost Recovery System, sales and exchanges, the use of partnerships, special accounting methods, investment tax credits and certain tax traps.

ACRS

The Economic Recovery Tax Act of 1981 completely revamped tax accounting for capital expenditures. Rules requiring depreciation of property over its useful life were replaced with a new Accelerated Cost Recovery System (ACRS).

Under ACRS, the cost of depreciable property is recovered over a specified period of time which is less than its economic useful life. Salvage value is also ignored. As a result, the period for

depreciating property has been shortened, and arguments between tax payers and the Internal Revenue Service over useful
lives have been eliminated. ACRS also applies to different periods
and rates for depreciation to different types of property. Although
tax proposals have been advanced to extend the number of ACRS
years, the concept of predetermined depreciation periods is likely
to remain unchanged. Some of the more significant provisions are
summarized below.

ACRS on Real Property

When ACRS was initially enacted, ACRS allowed taxpayers to
depreciate buildings and other improvements to real property over
a period as short as 15 years. In its move to generate additional tax
revenues in the Tax Reform Act of 1984, Congress lengthened that
period to 18 years. These changes are effective generally for property acquired after March 15, 1984. However, this longer recovery
period is still significantly shorter than the 30 to 50 year economic
life of a building that was previously used. The significant decrease
in the period for depreciating real property has increased deductions from real estate operations in the early years of the investment. The resulting tax savings have provided additional capital to
developers. In addition, large and small investors have been even
more attracted to real estate as an investment and have increased
their participation in real estate ownership through partnerships
formed with developers and syndicators.

The investor may elect either the straight-line or the 175 percent
declining-balance method (200 percent for certain low-income
housing.) The straight-line method using the tables prescribed by
the Internal Revenue Service permits the investor to depreciate the
cost of the property evenly over its ACRS life. The declining-
balance method is an accelerated method of depreciation. The
following table compares the two methods of depreciation on a full
year-by-year and cumulative basis for 18-year property:

Year:	1	2	3	4	5	6	7	8	9
Assigned %:	9	9	8	7	7	6	5	5	5
Straight-Line %:	5	6	6	6	6	6	6	6	6
Excess % (Annual):	4	3	2	1	1	0	(1)	(1)	(1)
Excess % (Cumulative):	4	7	9	10	11	11	10	9	8

Year:	10	11	12	13	14	15	16	17	18
Assigned %:	5	5	5	4	4	4	4	4	4
Straight-Line %:	6	5	5	5	5	5	5	5	5
Excess % (Annual):	(1)	0	0	(1)	(1)	(1)	(1)	(1)	(1)
Excess % (Cumulative):	7	7	7	6	5	4	3	2	1

The declining-balance method is used until it is more advantageous to switch to straight-line to increase deductions. If the straight-line method of depreciation is elected, the developer has the option of depreciating real property over a longer period of 35 to 45 years. These options provide flexibility in planning the timing of depreciation deductions. For the tax year the property is placed in service, the deduction is based on the number of months the property was in service using a mid-month convention. For the year of property disposition, the deduction reflects only the months in which it was in service using a mid-month convention. (Special rules apply to low-income housing.)

The ACRS provisions included in the Economic Recovery Tax Act of 1981 and the Tax Reform Act of 1984 are extremely complex. These Acts include special transitional rules for sales and exchanges of property, and special treatment for additions to property after it is placed in service. A careful review of these rules may yield planning opportunities available to developers in structuring real estate transactions.

Depreciation of Expenditures to Rehabilitate Low-Income Rental Housing

If certain requirements are met, qualified low-income rehabilitation expenditures may be depreciated using straight-line depreciation over a 60-month period with no salvage value. The maximum amount of qualifying expenditures subject to this is $40,000 a unit. The part of cost basis that is not depreciated using the 60-month method, is depreciated under ACRS.

The following conditions must be met for rehabilitation expenditures to qualify for these tax breaks:

- The expenses are made under a certified governmental program.
- The development costs are certified.
- The tenants occupy the units as principal residences, and the program provides for the sale of units to tenants who demonstrate home-ownership responsibility.
- The leasing and sale of the units are under a program in which the total taxable income from the leasing of each unit, and the amount realized on the sale of a unit, normally don't exceed the excess of (1) the taxpayer's cost basis for the unit (before adjustments for the deductions under Section 167), over (2) the net tax benefits to the taxpayer (consisting of the deductions under Section 167 less the tax incurred on the income from leasing).
- Expenditures are incurred after July 24, 1969, and before January 1, 1987.

If property qualifies for this depreciation method, 100% of the cost of the rehabilitation is deducted ratably over five years. Approximately 40% of the rehabilitation would be deducted in the first five years if the property were depreciated using the declining balance method and an 18 year life. The use of the straight-line method would result in approximately 29% of the expenditures being deducted in the first five years.

ACRS on Personal Property

Real estate frequently includes property that is classified as personal property for tax purposes. Most personal property associated with real estate is subject to cost recovery depreciation over a 5-year period using half-year convention. The prescribed percentages for personal property are based on the 150 percent declining-balance method, shifting to the straight-line method when that method produces larger deductions. Alternatively, the developer may elect straight-line depreciation. Property subject to 5-year recovery includes assets such as furniture, appliances, and carpeting.

Sales and Exchanges

Many tax planning opportunities are available on the disposition of real property. The following paragraphs discuss the tax implications of various methods of disposition and the pitfalls and planning opportunities associated with each method.

Sales of Real Property Held as Inventory

In general, gain from the sale of property held *for sale* to customers in the ordinary course of a taxpayer's trade or business is treated as ordinary income for tax purposes. This distinction is significant because long-term capital gains are taxable at lower tax rates (as discussed in the next section). However, gains from sales of property held *for investment* or for use in a trade or business are generally treated as capital gains.

In determining whether sales of real property are made in the ordinary course of a trade or business, the Courts look to the intent of the taxpayer in holding the property. In simple terms, a dealer is anyone who holds property primarily for sale to customers in the ordinary course of a trade or business. An investor is a passive owner of property who holds it for future appreciation in value. An investor may also hold property for its current income-producing potential.

In many cases, the distinction between dealer and investor property is unclear, which has caused a substantial amount of litigation. Sometimes a taxpayer may be a dealer with respect to one property and an investor with respect to a different property. Careful planning is required to ensure that capital gain treatment will be accorded to sales of property held for investment in these cases.

Sales of Property Held for Investment

As mentioned earlier, gain from the sale or exchange of real estate held for investment or for use in a trade or business is generally treated as a capital gain. If the property has been held for more than six months (one year in the case of real property held for investment and purchased before June 22, 1984), the gain is taxed at favorable long-term capital gain rates. For noncorporate taxpayers, only 40% of the gain is taxed, resulting in a maximum tax rate of 20% on the gain. Corporate taxpayers are taxed at a rate of 28% on long-term capital gains. A "Minimum Tax" may result from this preference and could increase the final tax owed. A section later in this chapter will explain details of the minimum tax concept.

Recapture

A portion of the taxable gain recognized from the sale of depreciable assets used in a trade or business may be taxed as ordinary income rather than as capital gain. This is commonly known as "depreciation recapture." The lesser of (1) the amount of the gain or (2) the amount of depreciation recapture is taxed as ordinary income. The amount of depreciation recapture is dependent upon the type of property and the method of depreciation used. The table included below illustrates the manner in which the depreciation recapture is computed.

TYPE OF PROPERTY	METHOD OF DEPRECIATION	AMOUNT OF DEPRECIATION RECAPTURE
Residential and Commercial Real Property	Straight-Line	None
Commercial Real Property	Accelerated	100% of Depreciation Deductions
Residential Real Property	Accelerated	Difference between Accelerated Depreciation and Straight-Line Depreciation
Personal Property (i.e., Furniture and fixtures, autos, etc.)	Accelerated and Straight Line	100% of Depreciation Deductions

In addition, if real property is held by a corporation, 20% of any depreciation that is not recaptured under the rules discussed above must be recaptured as if the property were personal property.

The following example illustrates the computation of depreciation recapture on the sale of residential real property for which an accelerated method of depreciation was used.

EXAMPLE: Mr. H. purchased an apartment complex on January 1, 1985, and elected to depreciate it over 18 years using accelerated depreciation rates. The land and building were purchased for $120,000 and Mr. H. deducted depreciation in the amount of $26,000. If he had elected the straight line method of depreciation, he would have deducted $17,000 of depreciation. Subsequently, Mr. H. sells the property for $150,000. His gain is computed as follows:

Sales Price:		$150,000
Basis:		
Purchase Price	$120,000	
Depreciation	(26,000)	(94,000)
Gain:		$56,000
Depreciation Recapture:		
Accelerated depreciation	$26,000	
Straight line depreciation	(17,000)	
Total depreciation recapture	$9,000	
Total Gain		$56,000
Less: Depreciation recapture taxed as ordinary income		(9,000)
Capital Gain		$47,000

As will be discussed later in this chapter, the ability to elect different methods of depreciation provides planning opportunities with respect to the timing of deductions and the type of gain to be recognized in the sale of property.

Installment Sales

In general, gain realized on the sale of property may be deferred when an installment note is received by the seller. The seller may report as income only the proportion of the installment payment received in each year that the gross profit bears to the selling price. For example: Mr. H. owned land that originally cost $100,000 and which he sold for $200,000 in 1986. Under the terms of the sales agreement, Mr. H. will collect $20,000 in 1986, and $20,000 plus interest in each succeeding year. In 1986, he will recognize gain of $10,000 computed as follows under the installment method:

Gross Profit Percentage:

$$\frac{\text{Cost of } \$100,000}{\text{Sales Price of } \$200,000} = 50\%$$

Gain Recognized in 1986:

Amount Received times Gross Profit Percentage = $10,000

Special rules apply where the purchaser takes property subject to or assumes a mortgage. The rules may cause immediate income recognition where the amount of the mortgage is greater than the tax basis of the property sold. In addition, if the property has ordinary income due to depreciation recapture, the developer must recognize such income at the time of sale, even though he does not receive cash. Because of these potential traps for the unwary, planning is required to time income recognition and to ensure that sufficient cash is received at the time of sale to pay the tax attributable to the depreciation recapture income.

Like-Kind and Deferred Exchanges

In some instances, the developer may wish to sell one property and use the proceeds to acquire another property. The recognition of part or all of the gain inherent in the property to be sold may be deferred for tax purposes by entering into a like-kind exchange. In that case, the developer would exchange his property for the property he wishes to acquire, thereby deferring the payment of tax on any gain inherent in his property. An exchange of an interest in real property for an interest in other real property qualifies as a tax-free like-kind exchange. An interest in real estate includes land, buildings, working interests in oil, remainder interests in real property, and leasehold interests with a term of more than 30 years.

However, it is often difficult to locate a purchaser for property who also has property that the seller wishes to acquire in a like-kind exchange. In these cases, the seller may require the purchaser to acquire suitable property with the money that would otherwise be used to fund the purchase. Then the purchaser and seller would exchange the properties with each, receiving the property he wished to acquire. These deferred like-kind exchanges of real property also qualify as tax-free exchanges if the exchange property is received within 180 days after the date on which the taxpayer relinquishes his property (or the due date of the taxpayer's return, if earlier) where the transferor designates the exchange property to be received within 45 days after the transfer. Because of these time limits, the transfer of the property should be deferred, if possible, until the property the developer wishes to receive has been identified and its purchase has been negotiated.

When the developer consummates a like-kind exchange, his tax basis (cost) for the old property becomes his tax basis for the new property, and the new property assumes any recapture potential associated with the old property. There is no recapture of depreciation on the exchange except to the extent of any gain recognized on the exchange. If the developer gives cash as part of a tax-free exchange, no gain or loss is recognized. However, if he receives cash or property which is not real estate, gain may be recognized based on the cash or fair market value of the non-qualifying property. If the other party assumes or takes the property subject to a mortgage, the debt is treated as additional cash received but is reduced by any cash the developer gives on the exchange and any debt he assumes. Therefore, he will recognize gain if he assumes less debt than the other party, such gain being limited to the gain inherent in the property.

For example, Mr. H. wishes to exchange an office building that is valued at $1,000,000 for a tract of undeveloped land valued at $900,000 and cash of $100,000. The building is subject to debt of $750,000 and has a tax basis of $600,000. Mr. H. will recognize gain computed as follows:

Gain realized		
Fair Market Value of Land Received		$1,000,000
Tax basis in office building		600,000
Gain Realized		$400,000
Gain recognized		
Cash received		$100,000
Debt transferred	$750,000	
Basis in office building	600,000	150,000
Gain recognized		$250,000

Advanced planning will enable the developer to minimize or defer the income to be recognized. For example, an installment note may be received rather than cash to equalize values. This allows the investor to defer the recognition of gain until the payments are received. This control over the timing of recognition of income will assist in the overall tax planning effort.

Partnerships as Ownership Vehicles

Partnerships are a favored vehicle for ownership of real estate by two or more owners. Because partnerships are treated as a pass-through entity for tax purposes, all income, gains, losses, deductions and credits flow through to the partners and are included in their returns. In addition, the partners retain flexibility in structuring and altering their economic arrangement. The partners' agreement with respect to the sharing of economic benefits, partnership debts, capital contribution requirements, distributions in liquidation, and operating and management responsibilities generally is documented in the partnership agreement. The partners may change their agreement between themselves at any time. This level of flexibility ordinarily is not available in a corporate structure.

Tax losses are typically generated in the early years of the ownership of real estate because of depreciation and interest deductions. These losses are deductible by the partners to the extent of their tax basis in assets contributed to the partnership and their share of partnership liabilities, including nonrecourse liabilities for which they have no personal responsibility, such as a mortgage on real estate. All other investments or activities, whether held inside or outside a partnership, are subject to additional limitations, known as the "at risk" limitations, on losses incurred. Under the "at risk" provisions which apply to investments other than real estate, losses are currently deductible only to the extent the taxpayer has amounts "at risk." You are considered "at risk" in an investment to the extent of your cash contribution, the adjusted basis of property you contribute and any amounts borrowed for use in the activity for which you are either personally liable or have pledged property held outside of the activity to the extent of its net fair market value. Because you may deduct losses in excess of your amount "at risk," real estate is an attractive investment for many investors.

Developers and syndicators often form limited partnerships to raise the capital required to construct or acquire commercial real estate. In a limited partnership, the limited partner is liable to the partnership and, indirectly its creditors, only to the extent of the capital he agrees to contribute. The fact that a limited partner's risk is limited to his investment makes the limited partnership an excellent investment vehicle for passive investors. Limited partners may be allocated a share of the partnerships' nonrecourse debt and may, therefore, deduct losses in an amount in excess of the capital they are obligated to contribute. The ability to allocate losses to and limit the liability of investors has made the limited partnership a favored vehicle for attracting necessary capital.

Partners may wish to allocate taxable income or loss or items of income, gain, deduction, or loss in a manner different than their overall sharing ratios. For example, depreciation, gain and loss on a particular asset may be allocated disproportionately to one or more partners. Such allocations are permitted only if the allocation has substantial economic effect. An allocation generally has substantial economic effect if the partner receiving the allocation will bear the economic benefit or burden of the allocation. Because the determination of whether an allocation has substantial economic effect is a complicated and unsettled area, you should consult a competent tax advisor to assist you in the structure of allocations of taxable income and loss among partners.

Special Accounting Methods

The real estate industry is subject to certain special tax accounting requirements. Special rules apply to construction period interest and taxes, deferred payments for services or the use of property and original issue discount. The provisions related to original issue discount, deferred payments for the use of property and deferred payments involving sales of property were enacted in the Tax Reform Act of 1984. They are extremely complex and their impact on many transactions is uncertain. These provisions are controversial and may be subject to future changes. At the time of this writing, regulations have not been drafted to clarify the many questions regarding these provisions.

Construction Period Interest and Taxes

Interest expense and property taxes incurred during the construction period must be capitalized and amortized over 10 years, unless the property being constructed is low-income housing. The first year's amortization is taken in the year the expense is incurred. The remainder is amortized beginning with the year after the expense was incurred or the year the property is placed in service or is ready to be held for sale, whichever comes later. (Construction period interest for low-income housing is deductible in the year incurred.)

Deferred Payments for the Use of Property

Strict new rules were imposed by the Tax Reform Act of 1984 on leasing arrangements that utilize "deferred rental" payments or "stepped rental" payments. Previously, lessors reported rental income and lessees claimed deductions for rents paid based upon their respective accounting methods. A cash method lessor would include rent in income only as received. An accrual basis lessee deducted the rents as the liability occurred under the terms of the lease even though payment might not be due until a later period. Thus, the lessee would deduct rental expense as it accrued but the lessor would not report the income until a later year.

Concerned that taxpayers were entering into "abusive" leasing arrangements, Congress enacted legislation to close the "loopholes." New parties entering into leases after June 8, 1984, which call for total payments in excess of $250,000 and use a deferred or stepped rental agreement are required to allocate the rental payments over the entire lease period, based upon present value concepts. They must include in income or deduct the accrued rent and unpaid interest in the proper period, regardless of their method of accounting. These leases are referred to as "Section 467 rental agreements."

For example, Partnership P (a cash-basis taxpayer) leases commercial office space to Corporation X under a five-year deferred rental arrangement. The terms of the agreement provide for rentals of $60,000 per year. However, only $25,000 has to be paid annually, with the deferred rent to be paid at the close of the lease period. The new provisions will require that the parties recognize the present value of the $60,000 rental amount for each taxable year in the lease period. To the extent that the required payment ($25,000) is less than the computed present value rent, interest will be computed on a compounding basis.

Additional restrictions are placed on certain leases that incorporate a tax-avoidance motive. Furthermore, if property subject to a leaseback or long-term lease is disposed of, special recapture rules may apply to convert capital gain to ordinary income.

Because these provisions apply only to leases that call for payments exceeding $250,000, many leases will be excepted from the new requirements. For leases with payments exceeding $250,000, you should carefully review these provisions to determine their potential tax implications.

Deferred Payments Involving Sales of Property

Prior to the Tax Reform Act of 1984, interest was imputed on deferred payments involving sales of property unless an adequate rate of interest was stated in the sales agreement. If interest was imputed, a portion of each deferred payment was treated as unstated interest, with the allocation based upon the size of each deferred payment.

For example, on July 1, 1981, A acquired a building from B for $100,000. The terms of the sale required $10,000 to be paid on June 20, 1982, and $90,000 to be paid on June 30, 1986, with no requirement to pay interest. Under prior law, approximately $35,700 of the total $100,000 would be imputed interest, assuming a 10% rate. A, the purchaser, regardless of whether he were a cash or accrual method taxpayer, would recognize $3,570 in interest expense in 1982 (10/100 x $35,700) and $32,130 in 1986 (90/100 x $35,700).

The Tax Reform Act of 1984 provides new rules designed to recognize the "economic reality" of the deferred payment transactions involving sales of property. If the sale of property involved deferred payments occurring more than 12 months (6 months in certain cases) from the date of sale and the transaction does not provide for adequate interest, interest will be imputed at an effective rate of 120% of the "applicable federal rate." The deferred payments will not be subject to the new provisions if an effective interest rate of at least 110% of the applicable federal rate is provided. The accrued interest must be currently included in income and deducted by the parties involved in the sale, regardless of their method of accounting.

Using the same example as above, and assuming that the sale occurred on July 1, 1985, and that 120% of the applicable interest rate is 10%, the new law would require A to recognize the interest expense — $35,700 — in the following manner:

1985	$3,200	1988	$7,200
1986	6,400	1989	8,000
1987	6,600	1990	4,300

Certain exceptions are provided in the Tax Reform Act of 1984 and subsequently have been expanded. Because of the complexity of these provisions and the controversy they have generated, it is possible that they will be subject to future changes. One should carefully consider the effect of these provisions in planning the purchase or sale of property on an installment basis.

Investment Tax Credit

The tax incentives arising from investment tax credits also impact the real estate industry. Investment tax credit is available for investment in personal property as well as for certain rehabilitation expenditures. The credit for rehabilitation expenditures has dramatically increased the level of activity in rehabilitating older buildings and certified historic structures, thereby providing a much needed "face-lift" for older buildings in both urban areas and smaller towns. The following paragraphs summarize these benefits.

ITC on Personal Property

Investment tax credit (ITC) of 10% is available on tangible personal property with a useful life of five years or more. A taxpayer using the 10% credit must reduce depreciable basis by half of the credit. In lieu of basis reduction, the taxpayer may take an 8% credit. There is a ceiling of $125,000 on the amount of used property qualifying for ITC. No credit is allowed for property used predominantly for permanent lodging, such as apartment complexes.

ITC offsets the first $25,000 of tax liability of a taxpayer plus 85% of any tax in excess of $25,000. Unused credits are carried back three years and then carried forward 15 years. Some of the assets in a building which qualify for ITC are: elevators, escalators, carpets, special electrical, plumbing and sprinkler systems in a factory, fire extinguishers, movable office partitions, computers, and exterior lighting. To the extent one maintains detailed records of the costs of construction, one can maximize the amount of investment tax credits available.

Rehabilitation Credits

In order to encourage rehabilitation of older buildings, Congress provided a 15% investment tax credit for "substantial rehabilitation" expenditures on commercial and industrial buildings at least 30 years old, and a 20% credit for buildings which are at least 40 years old. An improvement is substantial if it exceeds the greater of $5,000 or the taxpayer's adjusted cost basis in the building. A 25% credit is available for qualified expenditures to rehabilitate certified historic structures regardless of whether they are residential or commercial buildings. Depreciable basis is reduced by 100% of the credit taken for rehabilitation credits and 50% of the credit taken for certified historic structures. With proper planning, the rate of return on investments in these projects is extremely high due to the availability of these credits.

Recapture of Credits

If a taxpayer disposes of an interest in investment tax credit property before the end of its recapture period, the property is subject to recapture. The recapture period for five-year personal property and rehabilitated real estate is five years. The recapture percentage is 100% for the first full year after the date the property is placed in service, and is reduced by 20% each successive year.

When planning the disposition of property, you should not overlook the impact of investment credit recapture. The tax implications can be significant and can be particularly important if the property is a rehabilitated building or certified historic structure.

TAX TRAPS

Two provisions in the Internal Revenue Code, which are the bane of real estate developers, are the alternative minimum tax and the investment interest expense limitation. These two provisions are extremely complex, and can impare the tax benefits available from real estate investment. If either of these provisions could apply, you should consult your tax advisor.

Alternative Minimum Tax

Noncorporate taxpayers are subject to the alternative minimum tax to the extent that this tax exceeds their regular tax. A tax rate of 20% is applied to taxable income that exceeds an exemption amount in computing the alternative minimum tax. Taxpayers who are likely candidates for the alternative minimum tax are taxpayers with substantial accelerated depreciation, long-term capital gain, and ordinary losses from investments such as real estate. Investment tax credits may not be used to offset alternative minimum tax. Rather, the credits must first be carried back three years and then carried forward 15 years.

Corporate taxpayers are subject to an add-on minimum tax. Preference items, such as benefits derived from accelerated depreciation and favorable capital gains rates, are multiplied by 15%. This amount is added on to the corporation's tax liability to the extent it exceeds the greater of $10,000, or the corporation's regular tax liability computed with certain adjustments.

Investment Interest

In the case of a taxpayer other than a corporation, the amount of investment interest that can be deducted is $10,000 plus the taxpayer's net investment income. Net investment income includes passive income such as interest, dividends, rental income from net lease property, royalties, short-term capital gains, and depreciation recapture from net lease property reduced by related expenses. Investment interest expense includes interest incurred with respect to property held for investment, such as undeveloped land, and net lease property.

Rental property is considered net lease property in two instances. If the landlord is either guaranteed in whole or in part against the loss of income, or is guaranteed a specified return, the property will be considered net lease property. In addition, if expenses other than taxes, interest, depreciation, and reimbursed expenses are less than 15% of the rental income from the property, the property will be considered net lease property. Where a tenant agrees to reimburse a landlord for an expense or for any increase over a separately stated amount of expense, that expense will be considered a reimbursed expense. Accordingly, if a lease is structured to pass-through substantially all of the operating expenses to the tenant, that lease may be treated as a net lease and the interest may be considered investment interest.

Because of inflationary pressures on operating expenses, many leases are currently structured as net leases to protect the owners from losses that might occur if fixed rents were charged. In these cases, investment interest expense is generated. Significant depreciation deductions can result in net investment income from the property being less than the amount of the investment interest. Thus, developers and investors may be unable to deduct a portion of the interest expense unless they have passive income from other sources. However, a straight-line method of depreciation could be selected in place of an accelerated method, thereby increasing net investment income to allow deductions for investment interest. You should consider these provisions when structuring lease agreements and when investing in a project that has net leases to maximize the current deductibility of the interest expense.

EXAMPLE OF THE EFFECT OF TAX INCENTIVES

The following example illustrates the economic impact of tax incentives available after the Tax Reform Act of 1984 on a typical commercial real estate project. The first illustration computes the internal rate of return after federal income tax assuming certain tax incentives are available. The second illustration assumes that these incentives are not available. This comparison highlights the economic benefits attributable to the tax incentives. Assumptions incorporated in the example are provided below.

Assumptions

A developer has created plans for the construction and operation of a commercial office building. The project will be financed with an investment of $250,000 and construction financing of $4,750,000 which will be replaced with permanent financing upon completion of construction. The construction financing bears interest at a rate of 15%. The permanent financing bears interest at a rate of 14% and will be amortized over a 30-year period. Financing costs and construction period interest and taxes are incurred in the amounts of $95,000 and $362,250, respectively. The land is acquired and construction commences in January, 1986. The building is sold on December 31, 1990 for $5,250,000.

PROJECTED RESULTS WITH TAX INCENTIVES
With Tax Benefits

Income	1986	1987	1988	1989	1990	Total
Rent		$700,000	750,000	800,000	850,000	3,100,000
Gain on Disposal					1,451,166	1,451,166
Total Income	0	700,000	750,000	800,000	2,301,166	4,551,166
Expense (Non-Cash)						
Depreciation -Building		209,915	219,042	219,042	219,042	867,041
Depreciation —						
Furniture and Fixtures		15,000	22,000	21,000	0	58,000
Amort — Construction Period						
Interest and Taxes	36,225	36,225	36,225	36,225	36,225	181,125
Amortization -Finance Fee	3,167	3,167	3,167	3,167	82,332	95,000
Total Non-Cash Expense	39,392	264,307	280,434	279,434	337,599	1,201,166
Expense (Cash)						
Interest		664,308	662,654	660,754	658,571	2,646,287
Insurance		8,000	8,480	8,989	9,528	34,997
Professional		5,000	5,300	5,618	5,955	21,873
Repairs and Maintenance		12,000	12,720	13,483	14,292	52,495
Property Taxes		40,000	42,400	44,944	47,641	174,985
Utilities		25,000	26,500	28,090	29,775	109,365
Wages		23,000	24,380	25,843	27,393	100,616
Administrative		9,000	9,540	10,112	10,719	39,372
Total Cash Expense	0	786,308	791,974	797,833	803,875	3,179,990
Taxable Income (Loss)	(39,392)	(350,615)	(322,408)	(277,267)	1,159,692	170,010

Cash Flow

	1986	1987	1988	1989	1990	Total
Net Cash Flow from Operations (Before Principal Payments)	0	(86,308)	(41,974)	2,167	46,125	(79,990)
Principal Payments		(11,069)	(12,723)	(14,623)	(16,806)	(55,221)
Net Cash Flow from Operations Tax Benefit (Payment)	0	(97,377)	(54,697)	(12,456)	29,319	(135,211)
ITC (ITC Recapture)	19,696	175,308	161,204	138,634	(144,496)	350,345
Net Sales Proceeds	40,000				(16,000)	24,000
Capital Contributions					555,221	555,221
Net Cash Flow	(250,000)					(250,000)
	(190,304)	77,931	106,507	126,177	424,044	544,355

Return On Investment

Internal Rate of Return   37.03%

Assumptions included above:

1. Construction period interest and taxes are amortized over 10 years.
2. Financing costs are amortized over the 30-year term of the permanent financing.
3. Depreciation of the real property is computed using an 18-year recovery period and the straight-line method.
4. Depreciation of the personal property is computed using a 5-year recovery period and the accelerated method.
5. Tax losses offset ordinary income from other sources otherwise taxable at a 50% tax rate.

6. Gain on sale of the property is taxed at the favorable 20% tax rate.
7. Investment tax credit is available on personal property, elevators and escalators.

PROJECTED RESULTS WITHOUT TAX INCENTIVES
Without Tax Benefits

	1986	1987	1988	1989	1990	Total
Income						
Rent		$700,000	750,000	800,000	850,000	3,100,000
Gain on Disposal					825,500	825,500
Total Income	0	700,000	750,000	800,000	1,675,500	3,925,500
Expense (Non-Cash)						
Depreciation — Building		98,569	98,569	98,569	98,569	394,276
Depreciation — Furniture and Fixtures		12,500	12,500	12,500	12,500	50,000
Amort — Construction Period Interest and Taxes		9,056	9,056	9,056	9,056	36,224
Amortization — Finance Fee	3,167	3,167	3,167	3,167	82,332	95,000
Total Non-Cash Expense	3,167	123,292	123,292	123,292	202,457	595,500
Expense (Cash)						
Interest		664,308	662,654	660,754	658,571	2,646,287
Insurance		8,000	8,480	8,989	9,528	34,997
Professional		5,000	5,300	5,618	5,955	21,873
Repairs and Maintenance		12,000	12,720	13,483	14,292	52,495
Property Taxes		40,000	42,400	44,944	47,641	174,985
Utilities		25,000	26,500	28,090	29,775	109,365
Wages		23,000	24,380	25,843	27,393	100,616
Administrative		9,000	9,540	10,112	10,719	39,372
Total Cash Expense	0	786,308	791,974	797,833	803,875	3,179,990
Taxable Income (Loss)	(3,167)	(209,600)	(165,266)	(121,125)	669,168	170,010

Cash Flow

	1986	1987	1988	1989	1990	Total
Net Cash Flow from Operations (Before Principal Payments)	0	(86,308)	(41,974)	2,167	46,125	(79,990)
Principal Payments		(11,069)	(12,723)	(14,623)	(16,806)	(55,221)
Net Cash Flow from Operations						
Tax Benefit (Payment)	0	(97,377)	(54,697)	(12,456)	29,319	(135,211)
ITC (ITC Recapture)	1,584	104,800	82,633	60,563	(86,934)	162,646
Net Sales Proceeds						0
Capital Contributions					555,221	555,221
Net Cash Flow	(250,000)					(250,000)
	(248,416)	7,423	27,936	48,106	497,606	332,656

Return On Investment

Internal Rate of Return	19.88%

Assumptions included above:
1. Construction period interest and taxes are capitalized into the basis of the building and depreciated.
2. Financing costs are amortized over the 30-year term of the permanent financing.
3. Depreciation of the real property is computed using a 40-year useful life and the straight-line method.

4. Depreciation of the personal property is computed, using a 9-year useful life and the straight-line method.
5. Losses offset ordinary income from other sources taxed at a 50% tax rate.
6. Gain on sale of the property is taxed at a 20% tax rate.
7. Investment tax credit is not available for personal property.

TAX PLANNING OPPORTUNITIES

In addition to the tax planning opportunities previously discussed, there exist opportunities in all phases of real estate development and ownership. During the initial phase of acquisition and/or construction of real property, the developer should consider the economic and tax benefits of various financing alternatives. When the property is ready to be leased, the agent might use tax incentives to induce major tenants to enter into long-term leases. Also, one should consider current and future plans for the property when selecting the method of depreciation for the property. As we discussed earlier, many planning opportunities are available for disposing of real estate. In the following paragraphs, we will discuss methods of financing and leasing the property and the factors considered in selecting the method of depreciation.

Financing Techniques

Capital for the acquisition or construction of real estate projects is available from both lending sources and equity investors. In many instances, you may wish to finance your project partly with debt and partly with equity. Your decision-making process will involve many factors including the availability of funds from lenders and investors, the control you wish to retain, and the economic and after-tax cost of the debt or equity to be acquired.

Debt Financing

The use of debt financing is an attractive alternative in many situations. The developer retains control over the development and operation of his project. Changing market conditions have encouraged lenders to be flexible in structuring the rate of interest and payment terms of the debt. Because of this flexibility, you may tailor the terms of the financing to meet the anticipated needs and profitability of your project. In addition, the interest incurred is deductible either currently or over time for tax purposes. Thus, the cost of debt financing is reduced.

In many situations, a lender may wish to enjoy not only a return on investment, but also benefit from the appreciation of the business of the partnership. This may be accomplished via an interest rate stated in terms of a percentage of receipts, or a share in the appreciation in the project, or either of these conventions in addition to a stated interest rate. Another alternative is the convertible debt instrument.

The effect of a creditor becoming a partner is that the associated liability becomes a capital contribution. This reduces the amount of basis to the other partners and consequently limits the loss pass-through. In addition, the "lender" may be allocated a share of the partnership's losses and credits. Payments made to the "creditor" would be considered distributions rather than interest expense. The creditor-partner must recognize his share of income from the partnership rather than the recognition of "interest" received. However, the advantage of obtaining capital gains treatment on appreciation participation, vis-a-vis ordinary income treatment for interest income, may persuade lenders to accept classification as a partner. In the case of the convertible debt instrument, some questions exist as to whether the conversion is a tax-free transaction.

The distinction between a lender and a partner ultimately rests on how well the arrangement fits into the mold of a loan. Factors considered include:

- Risk of Loss
- Standard of Contingent Participation
- Fixed Interest Rate
- Status of the Obligation Under Local Law
- Status of Contingent Interest Under Local Law
- Right of Conversion to Equity
- Lender's Control
- Termination of the Contingency
- Thin Capitalization

Because of the significant difference in the tax consequences to both the borrower and the lender, one should structure debt carefully to evidence the intent that the arrangement with the lender is that of a debtor-creditor. In all cases, professional tax advice is recommended if there is any uncertainty regarding the tax treatment of the debt arrangements.

Equity Financing

In many instances, financial partners wish to acquire an equity interest in the project rather than a creditor position. Because developers often are unable to benefit from all of the taxable losses and investment tax credits from their projects, they may allocate a portion of these benefits to a financial partner who can receive full benefit for them. As a result, the developer may be required to give up less of his interest in the project in return for capital than if he borrowed the funds from a financial institution. The loss of benefits to the developer should be factored in the decision of whether to finance the project with debt or equity.

To raise capital for the development of additional projects, the developer may sell part or all of this interest in the project to syndicators. Either large public partnerships or smaller private partnerships are formed with capital contributions from individual investors. To invest in these projects, a large portion of the tax benefits are allocated to the investors to attract their contributions. Thus, syndicated limited partnerships have provided developers an additional source of funds.

Contributions of Land by Landowners

An additional source of financing is the contribution of land by the land owner to a partnership in lieu of a purchase of land for development. The land owner has the opportunity to participate in future profits in exchange for the contribution of his property. The developer benefits in that no cash is paid or debt incurred to acquire the land at the inception of the project when funds must be devoted to construction activities. Many tax planning opportunities as well as pitfalls arise in connection with contributions of property to partnerships. Therefore, one should consult a tax advisor in structuring these types of transactions.

Lease of Land

Rather than borrowing the funds to acquire land for development, developers may also consider leasing the underlying land. In most cases, the property reverts to the lessor at the end of the term of the lease. However, the lease term is of sufficient length for the developer to realize substantially all of the economic benefit from his project. The lessee may desire to share in a portion of the profits to be derived from the operation and sale of the project in return for a lesser guaranteed annual rental. Care should be exercised to ensure that the lessor is not unexpectedly considered a partner for tax purposes because of a level of participation in the project significantly greater than normal commercial practices.

Sale/Leasebacks

In recent years, the sale-leaseback has become a popular method of financing. The owner of a property will sell the property to an investor and at the same time lease it back. The sale-leaseback permits an owner of income-producing property to convert a fixed asset into cash while retaining control of the property. The seller/lessee retains control over the property so that the investor/lessor never assumes the burdens of managing the property. The investor/lessor benefits from the depreciation he may take on the property. This type of transaction must be carefully structured so as to avoid classification as a financing arrangement for tax purposes.

OPERATING REAL ESTATE

During the operating phase of a real estate project, the developer should continue to consider tax planning opportunities.

Transfer of Tax Benefits to Lessee

A developer may offer tax incentives to lessees as an inducement for leasing the property. This is a particularly good idea where the landlord cannot currently use the tax benefits.

If there is new property or improvements qualifying for investment tax credits and the tenant is the original user of such property, the landlord may elect to pass through the credits to the tenant. If there are common facilities, such as elevators and escalators, the credit for that property is allocable to the original tenants based on the relative amount of rental space occupied. Investment tax credit on property located within the space of a particular tenant may be passed through directly to that tenant. Another method for giving tax benefits to the tenant is to permit the tenant to make the leasehold improvements. So long as the lease contract does not specify that the tenant is required to make the improvements, the tenant should be able to depreciate the improvements and take any related tax credits. If the lease term, including renewal options, is less than the ACRS recovery period, the tenant can amortize the cost of the improvements ratably over the life of the lease.

To attract major tenants in a competitive environment, developers may offer the tenant a participation in the ownership of a project. The tenant receives an interest in the cash flow from operations, appreciation in value of the property and tax benefits. The developer obtains a long-term lease for a significant amount of space and a tenant that will attract other tenants to the property. In addition, long-term financing may be more easily obtained. In summary, this arrangement may be attractive to both developers and tenants because of the benefits available to each party.

Accelerated vs. Straight-line ACRS

For the first tax year in which property is placed in service, the owner will need to make a binding election to use either accelerated or straight-line ACRS. Generally, most people elect straight-line for commercial real property so as to avoid depreciation recapture when they sell the property. If one expects to hold the property for a long time, the time value of money can make accelerated depreciation a better alternative. Therefore, an owner should project the present value of both alternatives in anticipating that the property will be held for a long term.

For residential real estate and personal property, one may choose straight-line depreciation if an alternative minimum tax position as the excess of accelerated over straight-line depreciation is treated as taxable income for purposes of the alternative minimum tax.

FUTURE TRENDS AND CONSIDERATIONS

Congress has shown a trend in recent years to decrease some of the tax incentives available for real estate investment. This trend is due in part to a view in Congress that some tax benefits have encouraged the formation of "abusive" tax shelters. An "abusive" tax shelter is generally considered an investment that has no potential for economic profit other than the tax benefits associated with the investment. Some also feel that real estate incentives have become too generous as evidenced by the substantial growth of tax shelters and the rapid, tax-motivated, turnover of real property. The need to increase revenue has also played a key role in the recent attention given to the real estate industry. Since increases in taxes have become unpopular, "revenue enhancement" has become the favored method for raising revenue. The need for additional revenue will impact not only the real estate industry, but other industries as well. There is also a strong trend to substantially revise the tax system to achieve tax simplification. So that an investor can better understand the trend of recent legislation, we will describe some of the "reforms" which Congress has enacted in recent years.

The alternative minimum tax was enacted (and expanded) as a mechanism for taxing taxpayers with substantial economic income who would otherwise avoid taxation due to special deductions. The tax applies to taxpayers who are deemed to have excessive amounts of "tax preference" items such as long-term capital gain and accelerated depreciation. The provision is not meant to discourage investments in real estate. Rather, it can be viewed as a minimum flat rate tax. The provisions for the alternative minimum tax were expanded in 1983, and Congress may further expand its provisions as additional "revenue enhancement" is required.

In 1984, the ACRS period for depreciating real property was extended from 15 to 18 years. The Committee Reports state that the change was made due to a concern that the 15-year period was too generous. The Reports state that while Congress recognized that the 15-year life stimulated real estate investment in a healthy manner, it also led to tax motivated churning of property as well as an influx of "abusive" tax shelters. Several members of Congress continue to feel that the ACRS provisions are too generous and support a return to the depreciation provisions in effect prior to ACRS. Under these provisions, real property was depreciated over its economic useful life (generally a period of 30 to 50 years).

There is also a strong feeling in Congress that the system of taxation should be simplified. Several different proposals for a flat rate tax for taxation of individuals have been set forth. The impact on the real estate industry of a flat rate tax of some sort has not yet been fully assessed. Nonetheless, the existence of a flat rate tax may lessen the interest of some individual investors. In addition, the system of taxation of corporations may be altered somewhat due to this feeling that the system of taxation is overly complicated.

Despite the crackdown on perceived abuses and the potential elimination of those incentives which Congress deems too generous, real estate will continue to be a good investment. Congress has always protected real estate from harsh treatment because it recognizes the important role it plays in our economy. Therefore, many tax incentives should remain, and any investor should continue to experience a favorable environment for real estate investment. Creative tax planning from the very start can result in maximizing the return on the investments.

Leslie Finks, CPA, is a principal with Arthur Young & Company, Dallas. Arthur Young & Company is one of the largest international accounting, tax, and consulting firms in the world.

Ms. Finks is a member of the Real Estate Syndications & Securities Institute, a member of Arthur Young's industry specialty team for real estate, the editor of the Firm's publication — Real Estate Alert, *and a public speaker for such groups as the American Society of Appraisers. She is also a member of the firm's specialty team for partnership taxation.*

Charles Wurtzebach

REAL ESTATE IN THE NATIONAL ECONOMY

Real estate and real estate-related decisions affect everyone's life on a daily basis. The purpose of this chapter is to review the importance of real estate to our economy.

Consequently, a broad-based approach will be emphasized. The sheer physical size of the asset will be mentioned in terms of acreage, use, and ownership. The abundance of the asset will be reviewed, as will its continued critical importance as a natural resource. This physical importance leads directly to real estate's financial importance within the economy. The relationship between real estate and the economy will be addressed by outlining the impact real estate has on our wealth, income, and employment.

Within the investment community, real estate has long enjoyed an important position. Historically controlled by a limited number of investors, recent trends have broadened the base of real estate ownership and investment. Millions of Americans now own real estate of some form. Real estate's importance as a wealth building vehicle is well known. This chapter will outline some of the reasons that real estate has gained such a prominent role in the investment portfolios of millions of Americans.

As we approach the 21st century, changes are taking place in our economy which will have a major impact upon the real estate industry. As we shift from an economic base reliant upon heavy industry to one led by services and information technologies, real estate will remain a major segment of economic activity. Urban growth patterns and employment centers will inevitably change, and thus real estate activity will change; however, the importance that real estate has enjoyed over the years will continue. In fact, real estate development promises to expand significantly spurred on by greater investment benefits/inducements than ever before.

REAL ESTATE AS LAND

A familiar phrase, often attributed to Richard Ely, is "under all is the land." This statement is almost absurdly literal, yet land can indeed be considered civilization's common denominator. While nations and people are separated by culture, language, and distance, we all inhabit the earth and use its resources. The land has always provided us with sustenance. Whether it be for food, shelter, fuel, or as our place of business, the land is our number one resource. Its value throughout history reflects that importance. The entire history of mankind chronicles how land has been fought over and defended time and time again.

The value we place upon ownership of land by man has led to many disagreements about how land's vast resources should be used. Decisions have been affected by our individual and collective cultures, and the results influence everything from our daily activities to our society's development. In fact, development of the United States over the last 200+ years, can be viewed as a series of major land deals! The original acquisition of Manhattan, the development of the Erie Canal, the Louisiana Purchase, the railroads, the Oklahoma Land Rush, Texas cattle drives, and the California gold rush have literally built this country.

Land: Abundance, Ownership, and Use

The United States, perhaps more than any other nation, is blessed with an abundance of land of all types. Farmland, great forests, the Great Plains, river basins, coastlands, natural seaports, and urbanized areas all contribute to our economy and society in general. In all, the United States encompasses approximately 2.3 billion acres. There has never been, nor is there ever likely to be, an absolute shortage of land. However, well-located land is definitely in short supply in many areas. What makes land well-located, and hence valuable, is a key part of understanding the real estate industry.

Land's developmental potential, and ultimately its value, is controlled by who owns the land, its geographic location and physical characteristics. The federal government owns about 33 percent of the total acreage in the United States. However, because a large portion of this land is located in Alaska and other remote areas, the value of federal land is much less than 33 percent of the total value. State and local governments own another 8 percent, and Indian tribal lands account for 2 percent. Of the remaining land, 3 percent is classified as urban, i.e., developed or immediately developable land. This leaves 54 percent of the total acreage as privately-owned rural land.

When examining land use, the following breakdown results. Commercial and industrial sites account for approximately 3 percent of the total land in the United States. This category would incluae office buildings, shopping centers, warehouses, factories, and government buildings. Housing sites utilize about 2 percent of the total acreage available. Single-family dwellings, apartments, and residential condos would be included in this category. The remaining 95 percent of the total acreage is taken up by agricultural and forestry uses.

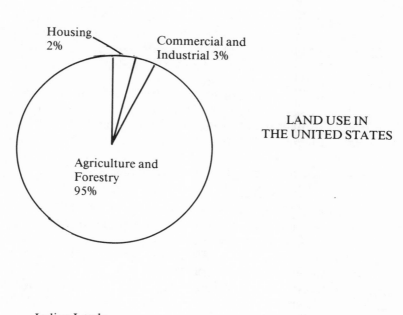

LAND USE IN
THE UNITED STATES

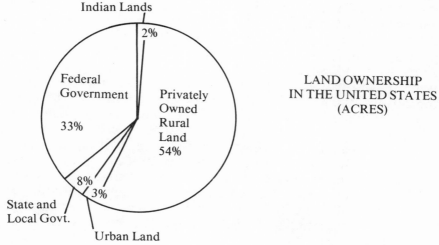

LAND OWNERSHIP
IN THE UNITED STATES
(ACRES)

Relatively speaking, our land use patterns focus on small, densely developed cities and large, open spaces despite any generalized description of our great cities as sprawling urban areas. While such statements are accurate when comparing U.S. metropolitan areas to many European cities, one finds that European countries do not have the vast land resources with which we have been blessed.

REAL ESTATE AS BUSINESS

Real estate has always played a significant role in the U.S. economy because it affects nearly every aspect of American business and government. Companies of all sizes utilize real estate and many now view this asset category as a major contributor to their overall balance sheet.

The impact of real estate upon the U.S. economy can be examined from several perspectives. First, real estate activity has a significant impact upon Gross National Product (GNP), national income, and employment. Secondly, real estate has long been viewed as an attractive investment vehicle; consequently, it becomes an important part of the estate planning process.

Real Estate and the Gross National Product

The Gross National Product (GNP), a measure of the value of the goods and services created by a given economy, amounted to some $884.1 billion dollars in 1983. Real estate accounted for $69.8 billion dollars or 7.95% of the entire GNP, making it the largest single industrial component of our economy. Residential and commercial construction comprise the major share of real estate's influence upon GNP. This category also includes thousands of individuals involved in marketing, leasing, and management of real estate. Historically, real estate investment, development, and services have actually accounted for about 10 percent of our GNP. As such, *real estate represents the largest single industry component within our economy.* On the consumption side, individuals consume about two-thirds of the GNP while the various levels of government purchase about twenty percent. The remaining 14-16% is reinvested in the economy by households via savings and private corporations via reinvestment. This reinvestment must be noted because it has a significant impact upon the nation's productive capacity in the future. Private investment must first be sufficient to provide for replacement of existing depreciated assets and second, must provide for new investment if the nation's productive capacity is to improve. Increases in the nation's productive capacity result in an increase in society's wealth.

On the consumption side of GNP, it is also important to note that more than half of our annual domestic private investment is in real estate. In 1983, Gross Private Domestic Investment topped $132.1 billion or 15-16% of total consumption. Residential housing investment ($34.8 billion) plus non-residential investment ($35.0 billion) represented about 50% of this total. (These figures do not include government investment in real estate.) As the largest component of gross private domestic investment, real estate plays a major role influencing the nation's productive capacity and society's wealth.

Real Estate and National Income

Examining national income provides another view of the relative importance of the real estate industry. It is essentially GNP minus depreciation and indirect business taxes. The two major components of national income that are real estate related are rent and interest. The different components of national income are listed as follows:

- *Compensation of Employees,* represents about 75% of the total GNP and has been generally increasing over the past two decades.
- *Corporate profit,* today represents about 8 to 10 percent and has been decreasing over the past two decades.
- *Proprietor's income,* represents about 5 to 6 percent of the total and has been decreasing.
- *Rent,* is about 3 to 4 percent and decreasing.
- *Interest,* is about five percent and has been increasing.

A particularly interesting relationship exists between the last two items, which has effected powerful new roles in the real estate industry. Two decades ago, rent was nearly three times interest, whereas today they are almost equal. This leveling off occurred because interest rates have risen more rapidly than rents. Also, as real estate values have risen over the past two decades the use of debt has also increased. Borrowed capital has increased as a percentage of the total financing for real estate investment, and more of the total cash flow has gone to lenders. As a result, lenders have gradually been obtaining a more active voice in decision making in the real estate industry.

Over the past few years, inflation and interest rates have subsided somewhat and interest should not continue to increase as rapidly as it did in the late 70s and early 80s. However, lenders will probably continue to have a significant impact upon real estate decision making, because of new freedoms gained under deregulation in the last few years. Financial institutions, that were previously limited primarily to the role of "pure" lenders, have now become more involved in real estate development, investment, and operation.

Employment

A third way to come to grips with the scope of the real estate industry is to look at national employment figures. Out of approximately 100 million workers employed in the United States, one million are employed in the real estate industry. This category includes real estate brokerage, leasing, property management, appraisal, and developers. Another four million workers are employed in the related construction industry. Thus, an impressive 5 percent of total U.S. employment is represented by real estate. No wonder government bureaucrats at all levels are so politically sensitive to proposed new developments and construction projects.

Frequently, local, state, and federal governments have supported policies directed at the real estate industry to turn the economic crisis around. Because debt has been traditionally used so extensively in real estate, the level of interest rates has a significant impact upon the level of construction and hence the overall activity of the economy. When interest rates are high or rising, construction starts are generally slow and construction workers are laid off. This leads to layoffs in other complementary fields, such as the lumber and the appliance industries. In many instances, economic recovery has been led by a rebound in housing construction stimulated by a reduction in interest rates.

In terms of social policy, federal, state, and local governments are the largest landlords in the country. Public housing accounts for the bulk of this ownership. Favorable tax policy has also been used as a public policy tool by government. The deductibility of mortgage interest, real estate taxes, and depreciation have made real estate a tax favored investment. Consequently, real estate has been identified as the most sought after investment and has become a major factor in wealth accumulation for corporations and individuals alike.

REAL ESTATE AND WEALTH BUILDING

Millions of Americans recognized real estate's importance as a major wealth building vehicle beginning in the 1960's. This contrasted with the long standing belief that real estate was a wealth building vehicle exclusively for the rich. Home ownership, real estate partnership investment, and real estate Individual Retirement Accounts (IRAs) have become popular real estate investments many Americans now include in their personal portfolios.

Home Ownership

Historically viewed, primarily as a preferred method of providing shelter, home ownership began to evolve as an investment vehicle during the middle and late 1960s. The factors which contributed to this change in consumer behavior were the demographic characteristics of the population and financial reality. As the "baby boomers" began to reach their prime homebuying years (25-40), the demand for housing increased dramatically.

At the same time, the financial situation heavily favored users of long-term debt. Specifically, as prices rose faster than interest rates, the real cost of debt declined and even became negative. Under such circumstances, borrowers were rewarded relative to lenders, and homeowners dramatically increased their use of debt. As home prices began to rise, Americans everywhere began to view their homes primarily as investments and secondarily as shelter. This wave of rising home prices and attractively priced debt continued over a decade until the late 70s.

The result of this tremendous interest in home ownership led to its identification as the symbol of the "American Dream." While fewer than 50 percent of all households lived in single-family dwellings prior to 1950, over two-thirds of the households did so by 1980 giving the United States the highest home ownership rate in the world.

This "home as investment" view has had a significant effect upon the real estate investment community. As individual homeowners began to recognize the attractiveness of home ownership as an investment, they also began to consider other types of real estate as viable investment alternatives. Rent houses, duplexes, fourplexes, apartment houses, etc., suddenly caught the eyes of investors. Faced with escalating income (and income taxes), individuals began to recognize the tax sheltering aspects of real estate ownership. Homeowners learned quickly that in addition to capital gain potential, the extensive use of debt in financing real estate resulted in large interest deductions. Primarily through this interest deduction, thousands of taxpayers began to claim itemized deductions on their tax returns.

However, real estate has always had several major drawbacks for the "average" investor. These drawbacks included the great amount of capital generally needed to invest, the expertise necessary to locate and select prime real estate, and the knowledge required to operate income property successfully. In an effort to overcome these drawbacks, real estate professionals developed real estate ownership vehicles designed to attract the "average" investor to real estate. The age of the real estate partnership was born.

Partnerships

During the 1970s and 80s, real estate partnerships have emerged as the primary method which allowed investors to overcome the traditional drawbacks associated with real estate investment. On the plus side, the partnership form of ownership allows for smaller equity contributions by individual investors, property selection by professionals, and professional property management. Furthermore, partnerships are not taxed at the entity level. That is, gains and losses are passed through to the individual partners. Personal liability on behalf of limited partners is restricted to the extent of their capital contribution. Consequently, partnerships provide very attractive tax planning opportunities with limited liability.

During the 1980s, real estate partnerships attracted a tremendous amount of attention from investors because of several key factors. Real estate had outperformed most other investment opportunities during the 1970s and early 80s. Federal income tax reforms continued to allow real estate's benefits of tax shelter. Finally, the deregulation of the securities industry heralded the entrance of Wall Street brokers as the premier marketers of real estate securities. As a result, both public and private real estate syndications grew dramatically, along with the surge in partnerships.

Real Estate Syndication

Real estate syndication has brought real estate investment opportunities to the forefront of American investment opportunities. Syndications of all types have been offered to investors and most have been accepted. Tax shelter-oriented syndications designed for high income investors, and cash flow-oriented syndications for pension funds and individual retirement accounts have been successful. It has been reported that the average real estate limited partnership formed between 1971 and 1978, provided an *after-tax* compound annual return of just over 10%. During the same period, the average *after-tax* returns from stock and treasury bill portfolios were about 5% and 3% respectively. The rate of inflation averaged 8% during this same period. Consequently, on an *after-tax* basis, real estate syndication returns tended to outpace inflation.

The real estate syndication industry has not limited its appeal to investors seeking tax shelters via depreciation and interest write-offs. Investors seeking cash flow and capital appreciation have also been attracted to real estate syndication. Small pension funds and bank trust departments have made substantial investments in the more conservatively structured all-cash syndications. Individuals have been investing in real estate syndications designed to be attractive for Individual Retirement Accounts (IRAs). In fact, many individuals are investing in income producing real estate for the first time by investing their annual IRA in real estate syndications.

Real Estate Individual Retirement Accounts

One of the most significant aspects of recent tax reform legislation has been the introduction of Individual Retirement Accounts. The purpose of this tax legislation is two-fold. First, it is designed to stimulate savings and investment. Second, it is intended to reduce future pressure on the Social Security system by encouraging the institutionalization of personal retirement funds. The law allows working individuals to invest up to $2,000 per year and spouses, not working outside of the home, to invest $250 *tax free* in a broad range of investment opportunities. Income earned on such investment is also not taxed until drawn out of the IRA. This opportunity has proven to be very attractive to many taxpayers.

Many individuals have invested their IRA's in real estate syndications, which frequently represent their first introductions to income producing real estate. While these IRA purchases are important relative to real estate investment in general, their major value lies in stimulating additional interest in real estate syndication, for investments above and beyond the IRA maximum. Consequently, the IRA legislation has benefited the real estate industry in two major ways: directly through the investment of IRAs themselves, and indirectly by bringing additional attention to real estate syndication as an investment alternative. These two factors should also broaden investment participation in real estate in general. Real estate's importance as a major wealth-building vehicle for millions of Americans, will only accelerate in the coming years.

REAL ESTATE AND THE HIGH-TECH ECONOMY OF THE FUTURE

Since the 1970s, the U.S. economy has been dramatically changing. This change can be summarized as a shift from a heavily industrialized economic base to a service and high-technology dominated base. Traditional industries such as steel and automobile production are no longer considered to be representative of America's leading production and economic centers. Heavy industry has moved rapidly into foreign markets as foreign plants have outperformed their U.S. counterparts. At the same time, the U.S. economy has been redirected towards service and high-tech development and production.

These economic changes have affected many facets of American life and real estate is no exception. Some of these changes have been subtle while others have had a truly significant impact on real estate development and marketing. For example, the incorporation of high-tech communication networks into new office buildings represents a relatively subtle change affecting the design process and the marketing function of developments. If tenants demand sophisticated communication networks, developers without such amenities in their buildings will find leasing increasingly difficult.

Beyond the amenities offered, the high-tech economy of the future has also significantly affected the mix and type of uses found in the marketplace. For example, the office showroom development is a fairly recent addition to the real estate market. As "business centers," these developments cater to a broad range of entrepreneurial businesses that prosper around a high-tech environment. In a broader context, the move towards service functions and high-tech development will have a dramatic impact upon urban growth, employment centers, associated housing, and the real estate industry as a whole.

As the nature of business changes, so will the nature of urban growth. A service and high-tech based economy will require a greater amount of office development relative to manufacturing plants. This means that urban growth patterns will be materially affected. A service/high-tech local economy implies a transportation oriented public infrastructure. This means that more highway and bus or light rail lines will be needed to transport workers to relatively densely developed office buildings and parks. Houston, Texas is a good example of such an economy. Dominated by office oriented businesses, Houston has developed an extensive highway system to deal with the traffic generated by workers traveling to and from work. Furthermore, Houston has expanded its bus system and introduced contra-flow traffic lanes and transitways to meet the peak rush hour traffic needs of its citizens.

The perceived impact of high-tech business upon growth can be seen as intense competition develops between cities and regions for the available supply of attractive employers. Nearly every region of the country, and for that matter, the industrialized world, is attempting to attract high-tech industry. Northern cities which have suffered the greatest loss due to the changes affecting the economy are now competing aggressively with Sunbelt states. Even states which have not been viewed as traditional heavy industry states, e.g., Iowa, are making aggressive overtures to high-tech businesses to locate in their state. As a result, not only are those regions which have begun to develop as high-tech centers competing with one another, but new regions are constantly entering the "market."

An excellent example of this competition was the attempt by several cities and regions to attract Microelectronic and Computer Corporation (MCC), a computer research and development consortium. MCC represents the joint efforts of several major computer companies which have agreed to cooperate in an effort to develop a new generation of computer hardware and software. Some thirty odd cities and regions throughout the U.S. attempted to lure MCC. After months of negotiations, MCC reduced the list of suitors to three diverse geographical areas of the U.S.: Austin, Texas; the Research Triangle of North Carolina; and the Silicon Valley region of California. Austin won out on the basis of, among other things, a complex network of incentives offered from the State of Texas, City of Austin, The University of Texas at Austin, Texas A&M University, the local business community, and others. The reason that MCC was so sought after dealt primarily with attracting new *high-tech jobs* to the region. The focus of attention was not on how many employees MCC itself would generate, but rather how many associated businesses would be attracted or developed as a result of MCC's choice of location. In other words, from an urban planning viewpoint, the key was synergism. Attract MCC and many additional firms would also choose the area.

High Tech and Employment Centers

The strength of any local real estate market is highly dependent upon the strength of the local economy. Local economic strength is a function not only of the number of jobs available, but also, and perhaps more importantly, the *type* of jobs. Jobs in growing, dynamic business areas are much more beneficial than those in stagnant or mature businesses. High-tech employment opportunities attract a young, highly educated, relatively affluent, motivated work force. These demographic characteristics have a significant impact upon the real estate industry. For example, retail, housing, and office warehouse/showroom markets are very favorably affected by a strong and growing high-tech work force. In short, high-tech means new jobs and growth which translates into many real estate opportunities.

SUMMARY

Real estate is at the very core of today's society. Real estate decisions affect every aspect of our lives. How we live, work, and play are all significantly affected by our real estate environment. Individuals, governments, and private businesses all make significant real estate decisions. As an economic force, the real estate industry provides jobs and an outlet for investment capital. The scope and changing nature of the U.S. economy directly affect the level and character of real estate activity. As markets and products change, the needs of tenants and investors change. In fact, it can be said that the one characteristic of real estate activity that remains constant, is change itself.

Charles Wurtzebach is associate professor of Real Estate and Finance at the College of Business Administration at the University of Texas at Austin. He has authored with Mike Miles, the well known real estate textbook, Modern Real Estate, *and has written numerous articles primarily on real estate finance for national real estate industry periodicals.*

Barry Henry

CREATING THE OFFICE BUILDING REAL ESTATE PRODUCT

The user (customer) should be the driving force in the creation of the product. Close correlation may be seen in all successful products in our society, including automobiles, clothing, computer products, etc. This is especially true in the creation and design of the office building real estate product.

The *needs* of the market for the product should influence all key decisions in the development process — where to build, when to build, what to build, how much to build, how to finance the project, and what price to pay for the land. It all gets back to what the user would pay to lease the space. It is the entrepreneur's (developer's) job to have a sensitivity to the market by being in the market and close to the customer. By staying close, the developer can properly guge the user's concerns and desires, and then develop a product of which the user, the community, and developer can be proud. Much like a doctor who is a trained expert in diagnosing what needs to be done for a patient, a developer must utilize his design/development team to address the needs of the market. This coordinated effort leads to what has become the orderly (and delightful!) development of our cities and communities.

There are different kinds of opportunities in any city and sub-markets within the city. A good developer will have a knack for determining what need or niche remains to be filled by the various product types he can build. The best and most successful developers are the ones who realize that the industry is truly *local* in nature. They sell with "proper sensitivity," and sell the prospect on their project.

When looking at the office building market in any city or any sub-market within the city during a generation of buildings being built, of say 4-6 new office buildings which is typical, it is interesting to note that there is always one, or possibly two buildings that are truly "special" and more successful than others. These are usually so special that they can almost lease themselves. Several factors have added this "special nature" to them:

- Location
- Design
- Superior or innovative technology
- Timing
- Price
- "Neighborhood"
- Amenities included in the project or nearby
- The existing tenant profile that will be in the building
- The tenant base that is the makeup of the area
- The strength of the sponsorship of the project (reputation, depth, capability, and service-orientation of the developer)

The more successful developers are the ones who create projects of this special nature and who are capable of gauging the future needs of the market. They always use the best talent, technology, and knowledge available to create the product. We believe these developers are often the ones who retain ownership, lease and manage the projects themselves, and who have an established tenant base coupled with an ongoing program of providing inventory/product. This type of program has real meaning to corporations and helps them make a "safe" decision.

STARTING THE PROCESS

Before determining where to build, why, and what to build and how much, let's look at where the process starts. First, a common element shared by most consistently successful developers (the leaders in the field) is their belief that the process cannot be done by an individual alone. The developer who is *close* to the market will start with an idea that comes from the market and put together an effective design/development team (whether in-house or contracted out) to design and mold the product for the market. Where to build and generally what to build is always a part of the developer's original idea stemming from the market, but he must have his team to add depth and to validate the assumptions.

The developer's team generally includes an architect, structural engineer, mechanical/electrical engineer, civil engineer and landscape consultant. The developer's job is to take a truly "hands-on" approach to the business and orchestrate the team's effort to create the product in light of his sensitivity to the market. The developer is generally the only one who can control the tempo, quality, budget and element of care and execution of the team — and it is imperative that he do so. He is the one who is at risk and will necessarily care more than paid outside consultants. We have seen far too many times how inattention to detail and lack of good execution can ruin a project that was originally well-conceived. Therefore, dedicated and experienced team members are essential to the project's success. They must be orchestrated properly throughout the process which can take generally from 12-36 months, depending on the type of product that is built and the area in which it is being built.

For best results, there must be a very good "chemistry" and working relationship between the team members. *Anyone* can build a project that is generally ill-conceived in light of the market, have it completed late, over budget, and have long construction punch lists that drag on forever at the end. All of this leads to severe tenant (customer) dissatisfaction — and eventually to the down-fall of the developer. The professional developer will design for the market at the right time, be on or ahead of schedule, be on or under budget and resolve quickly minor punch lists at the end — leading to a wonderful reputation and track record that comes back to the developer by repeat business, new business, and opportunity generated by word of mouth from satisfied customers.

THE WRONG REASONS TO DEVELOP

The product should not be created for the wrong reasons. The following are just a few examples of "wrong reasons." You can see examples of these in all cities and markets from time to time in projects that should not have been built:

- Do not count on your development to change the fabric of the neighborhood.
- Do not build just because there is capital available to do so — too many times we evolve to a capital driven market rather than a market driven market.
- Do not build for the egos of the developer or architect — build the best you can for the market.
- While a project should not be built unless it is quality, do not overspend on certain kinds of quality elements that will not be appreciated in some types of markets.
- Do not rely entirely on consultants — learn and study the details for yourself as well.
- Do not build a project based on market surveys done by outsiders — build from *your* sensitivity and familiarity of the market from being in it.
- Do not build something just because someone else with a good reputation has done so.

- Do not build unless you, yourself, are familiar with the market.
- Generally, do not put office buildings too close to industrial type neighborhoods without a residential base.
- Generally, do not fail to get user/customer input on design and concept.
- Generally, do not build projects without a discernable "front door" and logical site plan.

WHERE TO BUILD THE PRODUCT

Many potential mistakes in the development business can be avoided if the project has a great location. Where to build is an ever-present challenge to the developer in positioning himself in an ongoing and successful development program. There are many ingredients for determining where to build within the city. Some areas or sub-markets are obviously better than others. The following are a few factors to consider:

- Access
- Identity
- High profile site that can command good image and presence.
- Ability to draw from a wide, diversified and quality labor supply
- Traffic
- Proximity to transportation (mass transit, bus, taxi, air, etc.)
- Proximity to residential neighborhoods
- Proximity to, but not necessarily in the middle of, retail support services (hotels, shops, restaurants, copy centers, etc.)
- Quality neighborhood
- Available land at a cost and location that can justify the rents
- Proximity to clusters of larger corporate users who continuously have demand

It is best to be in a sub-market/neighborhood with an *identifiable-growth oriented tenant profile*. This includes an established tenant base, and one with a good history and image. A growth-oriented tenant profile several years ago was the oil industry. Today, some of the growth industries are communications, high technology, defense, service, insurance, and centers of entrepreneurial business activity.

The *existing* tenant base/profile is the most important element — from this is determined what niche to build to, what product, how much, etc. Good developers seem to have the capability of becoming an "industry analyst" of the users' industries. This helps the developer develop the right product in the right location.

WHAT TO BUILD

Once the developer has addressed where to build, he needs to address specifically with his design/development team, what to build. Again, this really must be driven by the market. There are generally six (6) types of office or office related products a developer builds:

1. Class A downtown or major urban high-rise buildings
2. Historical or adaptive reuse renovation projects
3. Class A (hopefully) mid-rise suburban projects (These generally seem to work best if they are of downtown quality, of large scale, etc.)
4. For lack of a better word, "low-rise/garden/campus type office projects"
5. Mixed use office, usually large-scale, coupled with retail, residential, hotel, athletic club, etc.
6. Build-to-suit type office projects to be either occupied exclusively by the user or mainly by the user

Generally, it seems to be best to build to the top end of the market, quality-wise. For example, that way, as is the indication of the hotel industry, if the market softens, you can always lower your rate and your building would lease more quickly than others. The market will more often than not, flock to quality and, in general, it seems most tenants in most markets prefer to be a small part of a larger project rather than a large part of a smaller project. The buildings that do the best are:

- ones that not only look good from the outside but function well and efficiently from the inside
- ones that are generally rectangular or modified rectangular in shape — lending more efficiency and flexibility to the user
- ones, style-wise today, that have a discernable bottom and top to the building form
- ones that have good finishes and attention to detail in the common areas
- ones that have effective and up-to-date life-safety systems
- ones that have real "people orientation" near the base of the building — outside, inside, landscape-wise, and in the plaza areas
- ones that seem to open outward on the first two floors or so, rather than inward
- ones that have a discernable front door and entrance
- ones that incorporate up-to-date building technology systems.

INFORMAL MARKET RESEARCH

In order to fully comprehend and diagnose the specific needs of the market, some developers utilize "man-on-the-street" type interviews with representatives of the various user industries. These people are those whose business judgement is respected and who may be tenants of the developer's. They include corporate real estate managers, prospective tenants, or just leaders in their respective fields. Basically, a developer will have several schemes or designs for the potential project done in renderings, models, plan or elevation form, some typical plans, site plan alternatives and color/skin/glass material samples and ask these people for their opinions. Opinions should also be obtained pertaining to retail and services needed in the building or area, ways to improve building management, trends in their industries that may dictate design modifications in the future, and countless other valuable input. If a developer and his team listen carefully, this information can help them create a project of "special nature" as was described previously.

TRENDS

Other trends have evolved in the development of the office product that are important to the developer. Typical floor sizes have grown steadily larger and more efficient since the buildings of the late '50's. These larger floor areas have proven to be better for the customer. Floor sizes in suburban projects tend to run generally in the 14,000 to 22,000 square foot range. Downtown highrise type projects run generally from 23,000 to 31,000 square feet.

Secondly, the trend is toward larger, not smaller buildings in general. In some downtown markets, many developers have made the mistake of building too small a speculative project. Smaller downtown spec projects seem to work, but only if they are built near major institutions that will continually help furnish overflow demand for space, or if they are situated on a permanent, special site.

Trends in fenestration are moving away from reflective-type glass, or even 100 percent glass. This is due in part to other materials being more cost-effective, such as granite, brick, etc.

Office developers are incorporating more and more security and life-safety systems and lighting in their projects. Major corporations and customers in general seem to have a desire for this.

Developers are spending more and more time, effort and money on extensive landscaping, which is a positive thing for the users. Along with this, many times, come fountains, sculpture, and outside seating areas, tending to make the exterior areas of the buildings more "people places."

Since users deserve more quality and service, the heating and air conditioning systems need to be state of the art, and provide for more tenant control and services. These features have caused people to dub these sophisticated new generation buildings "Intelligent (or, 'Smart') Buildings." There is a definite trend toward this in office building development in our country. Along these same lines, elevatoring in buildings is important to the user and should be studied very closely. The "under-elevatored building" historically will not do well over time.

There also seems to be a trend toward developing major office complexes using "name" architects. Many times, this can help in the marketing of the building as the architect's reputation and track record is identifiable to the users in the market. The customer can generally recognize and visualize other projects the architect has done around the country.

SUMMARY

Things continually change in the office building industry, but intuitions derived from being close to a changing customer/market will allow the developer to be successful over the long term. This, coupled with a caring and ongoing service oriented attitude will give to the user of the product what they deserve. The users of office space have become more intelligent and sophisticated and ask for, recognize, and deserve a better product and service from the development industry.

Barry Henry is a partner with the Trammell Crow Company, and is manager of the Dallas High Rise Division. This Trammell Crow division has been responsible for the development of twenty-eight major office buildings, which contain more than 12 million square feet. These high profile projects are built or are being built in Dallas, Fort Worth, San Antonio, and Washington, D.C.

Jerry Fults

MARKETING OFFICE PROPERTY

Back during the Great Depression, a poker-playing Bible salesman had just begun a sales tour through the Southwest when his car broke down in a sleepy East Texas town. With nothing to do for several hours while his Model A was being repaired, the Yankee salesman wandered over to the town's courthouse square where a small knot of men lounged on the benches.

"How'd you do, gents?" the salesman beamed. "Could I interest you fellas in a little friendly poker?"

After eyeing the tenderfoot for a moment, one stern farmer said, "You probably don't know it, son, but this is a God-fearin' town. There ain't no card-playin' here. It's the devil's work."

Recovering nicely, the salesman replied, "I'm glad you said that, mister. I was just testing the water. Over in my car I've got the finest leather-bound Bibles ever placed between a mother's hands. Now, if you'll just step over here . . ."

Like the Bible salesman, one might be able to spot the market quickly. But there's more to marketing office property than hit-and-miss market identification. In this chapter, we'll discuss where markets are located, their function, and their desires. And, we'll explore the organized steps to sell the market, from getting that first appointment to follow-up *after* the contracts are signed.

The three most important things about marketing office property, particularly in the Southwest, are: an understanding of the market, an organized leasing system to follow and enough flexibility to deal with any tenant at any level.

It is surprising that in today's era of pollsters, opinion-takers, and high-tech marketing techniques, there are still those who make little or no effort — or don't know how — to identify their markets. It's as if they grabbed a product, then leaped out the front door wearing a blindfold. And, unfortunately, office leasing isn't immune to the mistakes and fumbling of these careless, uninformed marketers.

LEASING SYSTEM

Without question, there are many different successful leasing systems. The program we're outlining here has been very productive for Fults & Associates. The system works because it provides an understanding of the market, and provides the steps to address the market.

For example, it's a joke to try to lease office space in the Southwest without giving a thought to the automobile parking problems and its solution. In New York City, it's not a major consideration because that's a pedestrian-oriented society. But in Dallas, Houston, or other major Southwestern cities, parking is still the major factor, in spite of current mass transit trends.

Leasing office space is, for the most part, selling location. And, like cars, or washing machines, or television sets, there are all kinds, sizes, shapes, colors, amenities, and prices. Let's look first at central business districts.

Texas is one of those states where, by law, there is no branch banking. When our towns were first built, they all contained the basics — a school, a church, a general store, a doctor, and a bank. Only the town doctor may have been more important, because the bank controls all the action. The town bank was — and is — the hub of all fiscal activity. Over the years, things have changed but the principles haven't. Lawyers, CPAs, hotels, newspapers, government offices, company headquarters — almost all of them have congregated around the town bank because they want to be close to the money, close to where financial transactions that affect them occur.

In short, central business districts were created long ago around money centers and the pattern never ceased.

Modern business has brought modern technology industries. These are more diverse than law, banking, accounting, or any of the service industries which have historically clustered around the downtown bank. We have, therefore, seen in the past 20 years a real proliferation of "office neighborhoods." Often, these are first populated by "clean", service-oriented, high-income industries and they cluster near the suburbs where white collar executives live and play.

There are, of course, other locations that can't be called downtown and can't be considered suburban office parks. These tend to be industrial and high-tech office locations which must be near their plants or industry bases.

In each case, in each location, whether it be downtown, suburban, or other, there is a common denominator which has fed growth and particular building activity. That common denominator is simply that business wants to locate where it does business best.

One can look at the central business district this way: money makes things happen. Where there is money, banks and lawyers can't be far behind. Money in turn, attracts accountants, which in turn lures restaurants and hotels — the circle widens. After location, decision makers must consider several other factors.

Experience dictates that a viable office building should have a floor "plate" of 20,000 to 25,000 square feet.

Secondly, a competitive office building in the Southwest must take into consideration how employees will get to work and what they'll do with their cars once they get there. Notice, we haven't mentioned subways, buses, cabs, commuter trains, or bicycles. The Southwest is an automobile-fixated society. If one wants to keep employees very long, and most employers do, then traffic and parking solutions for them are important. If an hourly employee must pay $50 a week or more for the privilege of walking several blocks to work from their parking lot they may not be employees very long. Again, it's no big deal in New York City, but it's important in Dallas, Phoenix and Oklahoma City.

There are many considerations of tenants in their decisions about location. For example, a hotel close by is the single best office building amenity. Additionally, tenants want places to eat, a bank, and convenient parking. Retail shops are peripheral amenities employees appreciate. Conveniences are something most employees have come to expect. Their employers — your client — expects them, too.

Tenants also want a good responsive building management. Clean, functional restrooms, good heating and cooling, security, clean windows, good janitorial service, a lobby that isn't cluttered, good lighting, and elevator service that works well are all important to the tenant.

It doesn't take long in the industry to realize there are developers and lenders who construct office buildings without giving a lot of prior thought and study as to who will occupy the building, and what services they will expect from it. One should clearly define and identify the market before attempting to lease space to that market.

IDENTIFYING AND QUALIFYING
THE TENANT PROSPECT

Surprisingly, 80 percent of prospective office tenants relocate within three miles of their present site. Relocating tenants look for a location which will serve their needs even better. The problem is to determine what tenants in the office neighborhood have done before and what it is they may be happier with in the future. The problem lies in identifying this "new business."

At Fults, we do a couple of things. We canvass tenants in the area and ask them, "Why are they where they are? What do they like about the area and what don't they like? What more do they need or want?"

Secondly, we do an "anatomy" of a building. We take a given building apart, tenant by tenant, studying who is already there, what is vacant, which tenants will need to expand or construct, and who will be forced to move.

This tenant by tenant analysis is necessary to identify "compulsion" — the thing(s) which require them to seek other office locations. It may be their present space is too small, or too large for their needs. And, there may be other annoyances.

Perhaps their building isn't managed properly. (Remember those dirty restrooms and bad lighting?)

It may be that the company has grown to the point where it's ready to have its own building — a place where it can gain building identity. The firm may be ready for an "ego" move to quarters that identify it on a number of levels.

Or, believe it or not, it may be that the boss just wants to locate closer to his home, or to his golf course!

Whatever the reason(s) for "compulsion", they are part of the "system", part of being organized in the sales approach. Another part of our system is the ability to be a chameleon, to be able to discuss with the prospect his needs in terms he understands, presented in ways which are clear and comprehensible and "friendly" — not challenging or authoritarian.

Remember, without an orderly, systematic approach that is followed each day, one will never know where one is in the sales process. If there is no frame of reference, the leasing agent will eventually flounder. With a system, this can be avoided.

Once one has identified the compulsion — the "want-to-move syndrome" — there are decisions to be made. First, can the prospect even afford to move to new quarters? Given the right economic opportunity, anybody will move. Can they afford it? A prospect will never become a tenant if they can't pay!

Finally, in determining who is a good prospect and who isn't, an agent must determine if the prospect is accessible. Without an entree, the leasing process is temporarily halted.

Here's a case in point. A few years ago a major eastern corporation decided to move its headquarters to Dallas. Everybody knew the firm had an identifiable compulsion to relocate. And there certainly was no question in anybody's mind that the client could afford just about anything it wanted. Two elements of our system were satisfied.

We tried every approach known with this major company, but we had no contacts there. No one could open doors for us. And having an entree with this company was an important element in securing the business. After a lot of wasted time and money, we concluded we had failed to get the proper entree. The firm used "friends" in New York to find office space in Dallas, and Dallas acquired a Headquarters Company. But it proved up the formula: one must have a tenant who *wants* to move; a tenant who can *afford* to move; and, just as important, a tenant that can be *reached.* In this case, we couldn't even get the door open. But, let's assume that all of the above requirements were met, now it's time to actually present to the prospect. The office "product" may be costly, complex and sometimes confusing to the client. This is an art into itself. Selling.

Although you are a chameleon, someone who can talk to anyone on their level and communicate effectively with them in terms they understand, the chances against closing the deal on the first meeting are very remote. Therefore, approach the job as a series of small sales.

THE SALE

The steps we follow, the things which work for us, are:

1. Identify the prospect's problem areas. Take inventory of the firm's current space requirement and determine what additional space they will need. Take into account their near term, future, and long range needs. This information is usually acquired by a series of "cold calls" and a space program.
2. Once the client's present position has been assessed, disturb him by pointing out problems he may not yet foresee, while acknowledging problems he already is aware of. Office tenants aren't aware of many of the problems of relocation because they are not accustomed to dealing with facility problems on a daily basis.
3. Offer a solution; your solution. The next step then is to show the tenant a building. The old saying, "life by the yard is hard, by the inch a cinch" is important in this step. Take your prospect along inch by inch.

We have already helped him see that he needs help. Now guide him toward a solution. Make a date with the prospect to look at office space in a building you feel will resolve most, if not all, of the tenant's problems. Do your homework. Know enough about the property, and your prospect's needs, that you can capably demonstrate how his needs and your solutions come together. There's no substitute for honesty. If the solution really doesn't fit the bill, admit it. Don't fudge. If the solution won't solve the problems, save the client more problems, and do yourself a favor as well.

There are two effective tools we frequently use when representing an owner in the leasing of a major office project. One is the multimedia presentation in a marketing center. Through this medium, we answer a lot of the obvious objections a client may pose and we handle this through a "third" person — the presentation. There is some good psychology at work here by having a faceless narrator supplying information. It creates a mood of better objectivity and helps illustrate the important points.

A brochure is the sales piece that ties the entire project together in a "carry out" form. It should be designed along the following lines:

- It is a *sales* piece; not a *mail* piece, therefore, it should tell a story in progressive steps.
- On the front cover, or near it, should be a picture of the project.
- The brochure should be done in a high grade of paper stock to appeal to the senses of sight and touch.
- Professionally designed graphics should be used.
- The brochure should incorporate pictures and illustrations of the project and its amenities, plus a thoroughfare plan, typical floor plans, elevator breaks, corridor layout, parking spaces, etc.
- Address and phone number of the property should be printed prominently, but discreetly.

The brochure, properly constructed, will be the reference point for future conversations.

4. The most tangible evidence of a solution to the tenant's problems is a space plan. By having a space plan done, we are getting the prospect involved whether he realizes it or not. When an architect produces a space plan showing where the tenant should put his office, or the computer room, the tenant's immediately going to make changes. It's hard not to because no one understands the business' traffic flow like the tenant himself. The client must visualize himself in that office building. He's moving desks and doors around on paper.

It is important not to be frightened by objections. Once understood, the selling process can begin. What may appear to be traffic congestion to one tenant is really high visibility to another. If your prospect is someone who needs and wants a high street profile, then all that traffic outside is working to his benefit — and yours.

With the proper homework coupled with several building profiles, the tenants may begin to surface due to the great detail used
in defining the products. There will always be prospects who need
solutions. It is not an agent's job to educate the client. One should
solve his problems.

Objections are part of the process. When a prospect says "no",
it generally means he has something on his mind other than a flat
rejection. Consider this moment to be the perfect occasion to be
quiet and listen. The client, as he talks, will open windows into his
mind. He's going to tell you what's really on his mind, what he
really thinks, provided he is able to talk without interruption.

He may have said, "No, thanks, there isn't enough parking
space." Don't walk away thinking, necessarily, there was a parking space problem. It may be the prospect is on the verge of
bankruptcy, or a move to a distant city, or really wants a Chinese
pagoda! Give him a chance to speak.

If there are serious specific objections, don't whitewash them. If
the prospect says the building management is ugly, make a note of
it and move on to other objections. Find out all of them. Children
handle objections wonderfully. They ask pointed, specific questions and listen closely to see if they are really answered. The rule
is to be simplistic in answers to specific objections.

If the prospect cannot be helped, say so. He'll appreciate the
candor and he'll tell his associates and friends. There may come a
time when a property might fit his needs. The next visit will be a
good deal easier, and more relaxed.

Part of the success of answering objections is knowing more
answers than there are objections. Make sure you've got more
facts than there are objections.

SUMMARY

At this point, let's summarize. In the beginning, we said
"You've got to have a plan, a system for tackling the
marketplace." Without it, there can be no measure of progress.
Morever, without a system, one won't be able to tell what actually
brought on success. Or failure.

Next, remember that chameleon. Use it to good advantage
when meeting and talking with clients. In his exchange with a
client, the agent must be able to switch gears smoothly to facilitate
an understanding of the client's needs and concerns.

When looking for tenant prospects, do profiles or anatomies of
other office buildings. The prospective tenants will begin to
emerge. Among these, identify those with compulsion to move,
those who can afford to move, and those with whom you can

develop an entree. This will yield a good customer profile.

Show the property, and develop the space plans which will get the prospect involved.

Face objections positively. Regard them as opportunities to sell. Selling is the name of the business.

Among the final steps is what is called "trading business points." If the tenant wants more parking spaces, the owner will want more rent money. The tenant wants vinyl covered walls; the owner wants to save on the interior finish. The tenant wants an employee lounge. The owner doesn't have to recarpet the reception area. All of these things are trade-offs so be prepared for them, as they are the heart of our business.

For example, let's assume a verbal approval between landlord and tenant, outlined in letter form. This is known as a proposal and is an important step before going to lease documentation.

Now that the office building is leased with tenants, problems can still surface. First of all, with a filled building one must now turn away prospects who are interested in leasing there. Secondly, there are those tenants who want to grow within the building or rearrange their layout so they have offices on the second and third floors rather than the first and 14th. No employer likes to see his paid employees spending a lot of their time waiting for elevators. Keeping them in your building under mutually satisfactory circumstances presents a whole new ballgame.

The theme of this chapter has been to organize a formula, a plan for locating tenants. And then stop, look and listen to it. Learn to listen and pay close attention to the details, in the immediate environment.

Donuts

There once were three donut shops on the same block. One had a sign which proclaimed, "Best donuts in the world." The next shop's sign said, "Best donuts in town." The third shop had a sign which said simply, "Best donuts on this block."

Be aware, but not too concerned with what's going on in other market areas or geographic areas. What sells in Miami won't necessarily sell in Memphis. Trends in Phoenix may never occur in Philadelphia. Look at the available office space and then look at the various tenants around it. One may discover that the donuts are exactly what they want.

Jerry Fults is president of Fults & Associates, an industry leader in facilities consulting, income property brokerage, and project leasing. Fults & Associates is exclusively marketing and leasing two major Dallas mixed-use projects which contain more than 3.5 million square feet of office space. One is The Crescent, which is adjacent to the Downtown Core. The Crescent contains 1,250,000 square feet of office space, the 226 room Rosewood Hotel, and 175,000 square feet of retail space.

Mr. Fults is a national lecturer for the Building Owners and Managers Association (BOMA International) and is the current recipient of the prestigious Stemmons Award.

John Bruemmer

BUYING REAL ESTATE

Last year, more than $60 billion was invested in new commercial real estate properties. This staggering figure does not even include money spent on existing commercial real estate properties.

The volume does not imply that buying real estate is a quick, cut-and-dried process. Real estate can be bought effectively, but it is a complex task. Prices are negotiable. Financing can be complex. Timing is critical. And you have to be farsighted enough to know if the property will stand the test of time.

To analyze the buying process, we will first identify the major buyers of commercial real estate — syndications, managed pension funds and insurance general account funds, joint ventures, entrepreneurs, and corporations — and show how they buy real estate. As we'll see, whether consciously or not, most buyers use a technique we call "buying by objective."

With this technique, the buyer begins with certain specific objectives. They could be cash flow, long-term appreciation, upside potential, tax benefits or even an emotional reason. Once the objectives are established, properties are sought to meet these objectives.

After analyzing the major buyers of real estate and how they "buy by objective," we will then examine the specific negotiating strategies and tactics that lead to the actual purchase.

SYNDICATIONS

Real estate syndications alone accounted for almost 27 percent of new commercial real estate purchases in 1983. That translates into more than $16 billion.

Syndications are so active because they allow individual investors to pool their money and make major commercial real estate purchases none could afford singly. The investors gain three attractive economic advantages: cash flow or yield, appreciation potential and an income tax shelter.

Guided by these basic investor goals, the syndication typically seeks an existing property that meets the following key buying objectives:

- Good debt coverage. It's the leverage of a first and/or second mortgage that provides the advantage of depreciation tax benefits.
- High yields. Syndications compete with other financial vehicles, although some yield is often sacrificed because of mortgage leverage and tax shelter depreciation.
- Good appreciation over the "hold" period. There must be good potential to increase the value through refinancing or releasing.

By buying properties that meet these objectives, the syndication can attract the funds by which they live and die.

Syndications must be fierce competitors for all types of properties; all are looking to satisfy the same three objectives.

While most syndications do provide safe, reliable investments and perform as expected, some syndications today also seek so-called "high-risk" properties. Here, the objective is a higher return for the investor. Consequently, he also assumes the additional risks of development: initial investment, financing, and the initial lease-up of the development.

A few examples of how syndications use their basic objectives to buy properties should illustrate the strategies involved.

A large insurance company with an asset base of $3.5 billion had taken back a 60,000 square foot office park in Atlanta on a mortgage default. The insurance company held the property for seven years as a passive investor, turning the management over to a local agent.

Due to certain internal earnings requirements, the insurance company decided to sell. We stepped in to market the property.

We found a relatively small syndication ($200 million) to buy the property. The syndication bought the property because it met their basic buying objectives.

First, the syndication was able to secure its tax shelter by obtaining market rate financing for a majority of the property's purchase price. Also, the syndication believed that through minimal capital improvements of about $500,000 the value of the property would be increased by $2 million. These capital improvements would include an upgrading of the building and grounds. Value could be further increased in the medium term by raising rents $2 to $3 per square foot, and securing larger tenants and longer leases.

This was a fairly simple and straight-forward transaction. But syndications often find themselves competing for properties —

and not just with other syndications.

Our second example pits a syndication against an institutional buyer. We like this example because it shows how different buyers have different objectives. It also shows how the buyer's objectives can determine the eventual outcome of the transaction.

A 60,000-square-foot office building in Austin, Texas was taken back by an insurance company in a foreclosure. It was one of five buildings in an office park. The other four buildings were owned by an institution. The institution wanted the fifth building so it could meet its objectives: good rental performance, a consistent marketing plan, and similar general appearance. The institution made an all-cash offer of $2.5 million to purchase the building.

We determined that this offer was far below the true value of the property and advised the owner to market the property and obtain a better offer. After all, buyers' objectives may vary, but sellers' objectives are usually to get the highest price within a desired time frame.

We found a limited partnership syndication who offered to buy the property for $4.2 million. And they did it because the property met their objectives.

The partners obtained a mortgage of $3.9 million on the building, supplying the remainder of the cost in cash. This large mortgage gave them the good debt leverage they desired.

Because the partnership offered such a high price, the seller agreed to guarantee a certain rate of return required by the investors for the first year.

The partnership hoped to lease the property within that initial year, eventually raise rents and then sell the property for a profit. The partnership's buying objectives were clearly defined.

The institution that made the initial offer had different buying objectives than the syndication. The institution wanted to pay all cash and quickly lock up a safe deal. While the buyer's objectives often determine the outcome of a deal, the seller's objectives must also be satisfied. In this case, the seller got a higher price by meeting the second bidder's objectives.

MANAGED PENSION FUNDS AND INSURANCE GENERAL ACCOUNT FUNDS

Pension funds are becoming a major buying force in commercial real estate. Last year, about five percent of all pension investment funds were invested in real estate. This figure is expected to rise to 15 or 20 percent of all available pension investment funds in years to come as funds better understand the complexities of real estate and its great potential.

Typically, the pension fund does not purchase real estate itself, but turns to an outside adviser — the pension fund manager. In recent years, large insurance companies have become one of the major buyers of existing real estate, by serving as purchasing advisers to managed pension funds. In the past, insurance companies used their general account funds to purchase real estate. Today, general account funds are used primarily to develop new properties. The next section reviews how insurance companies use their general account funds to develop properties through joint ventures.

Pension fund managers seek properties based on the general criteria established by the fund — whether it's a particular yield or appreciation potential. Pension fund managers also are very competitive among themselves — each trying to locate the best performing properties to meet the fund's buying objectives. Because one of the manager's fees is a percentage of the cash flow over the hold period of the property, he is particularly motivated to locate the best performing property.

The pension fund manager, acting as the fiduciary for the pension benefits of individuals, works with rather simple buying objectives:

- High initial yields. Reinvesting current cash flows should yield 11 to 12 percent at market value.
- Appreciation. Good upside potential can sometimes provide an internal rate of return ranging from 14 to 20 percent over the "hold" period (say 10 years) of the property.
- Safety. Properties are sought that offer high quality and good locations. The properties should not need capital improvements that will affect initial or mid-term yields.

Unlike the syndication, the pension fund manager does not seek a tax shelter. Debt coverage is not an objective; therefore, the pension fund is normally an all-cash purchaser.

The pension fund managers must work within the ERISA Act, a recent Pension Trust tax law. This Act requires that the fund meet certain standards (especially for safety). This has specific ramifications for real estate purchases.

For example, a fund must receive authorization from ERISA's regulatory body if a major tenant is a member of the fund that owns the property under consideration. The concern is that the major tenant, who indirectly owns the property through its pension benefits, could put the return of the fund in jeopardy by vacating the property. A conflict of interest exists as well.

Although competition for good properties is intense among all types of buyers, pension funds typically compete with each other for major properties. Managers are drawn to large, high-quality properties (in the $10 million to $200 million range) such as major regional shopping centers and major downtown office projects that are relatively new.

Managers also seek prime properties. As an example, the Pan-Am Building in New York City was purchased by a pension fund of Metropolitan Life Insurance for approximately $500 million. Managers have found that these prime properties compete very well in the marketplace over time. Smaller syndications and entrepreneurs usually are priced out of such major transactions — especially when dealing on an all-cash basis.

Here's a good example of how two pension funds competed for a piece of real estate in the $65 million to $70 million range.

A pension fund manager in New York City wanted a property in Chicago for its fund. It located two buildings on Wacker Drive that offered a total of 1 million square feet. After studying the marketplace, the manager recommended a bid of approximately $65 million.

A second pooled pension fund, with a local manager, bid $6.5 million more and purchased the property. The local manager had a better understanding of the marketplace, knowing that Wacker Drive was emerging as a business address on a par with LaSalle Street. In addition, the Chicago manager knew the buildings were underleased and could be increased substantially in value through a professional leasing program.

As it turned out, the pension fund made a wise purchase and was correct in its more aggressive market assumptions.

In this case, each pension fund had the same buying objectives, but it was the superior market knowledge of one of the managers that determined the final outcome.

JOINT VENTURES

The joint venture must satisfy the buying objectives of two or more parties. While each party has its own objectives, a joint venture is formed to benefit all parties.

In this respect, the joint venture is no different than a marriage where two people may have different reasons for getting married, but both benefit from the association.

Joint ventures in real estate typically involve an active and a passive partner. The active partner — usually the developer or entrepreneur — handles the development and management of the property. The passive partner — usually the insurance company or pension fund — is the financial partner. In most cases, the general account funds of insurance companies are teamed with individuals/developers and/or syndications to create joint ventures.

The developing partner has several objectives:

- Financial backing. The developer or entrepreneur needs money to create a new project or maintain a holding in a project.
- Tax benefit. Although the latest tax act restricts tax benefits in certain properties to equity ownership, there are ways for the active partner to receive a majority of the tax benefits.
- Fee Potential. The active partner seeks to earn a fee on the development of a property, plus additional commissions for leasing and possibly managing the property.

The financial partner has several objectives also:

- Project development. The financial partner wants to develop a real estate project.
- Cash flow. The financial partner is seeking a preferred cash flow position.
- Long-term appreciation. The financial partner seeks a project with good prospects for appreciation.

The objectives of both buyers are met through a joint venture, because each contributes needed expertise that the other lacks.

Institutional clients, for the most part, do not have the staffing or market expertise to create the value in a real estate product. Therefore, they pass that job on to an experienced developer or entrepreneur.

In exchange for financial backing, either through a mortgage/ equity or straight equity contribution from the financial partner, the developer assumes the construction risk and the risk for the initial lease-up and marketing of the project. Also, the developer gives a preferred cash flow position to the financial partner.

It should be noted that although legal documents can be drawn up to protect the financial partner, he will always assume some risk for the total project.

The following example shows how a joint venture benefited two parties with separate objectives.

A Chicago-area property offered a 20,000-sq.-ft. building, which was housing two movie theaters. The theaters were 20 years old and located in a growing and much sought-after suburban area. In a 10 year period, values on the land had risen from 50 cents to $8 per square foot. Obviously, the land was being far under utilized.

A large insurance company without development expertise wanted property in the area. The insurance company entered into a joint venture with a developer to build an eight-story, 230,000-

square-foot office building on the site.

The developer, as the active partner, offered the capability to develop, manage and lease the property. The developer assumed the risk of creating the product but not at the expense of encumbering his assets with the financing of the property. The developer also was paid a fee for creating the project plus commissions on the leasing and management of the property.

The insurance company, as financial partner, took a mortgage on the property for about 90 percent of the value. The financial partner also took a preferred cash flow on the balance of his equity contribution.

Here, the developer got the financial backing to create a successful project and made money. The insurance company made a good investment, while gaining expertise from an experienced developer. Both parties met their objectives. Both benefited.

ENTREPRENEURS

Entrepreneurs include all types of real estate buyers: developers, general partnerships, foreign investors, and individuals. They all seek capital appreciation over the long or short term.

Although entrepreneurs can vary, let's look at how the typical domestic entrepreneur buys real estate.

The typical entrepreneur is a domestic commercial investor with an investment range of $1 million to $20 million. He expects capital appreciation over a relatively short period of time — one to five years.

The entrepreneur usually has only two buying objectives:

- Financing. Assumable or obtainable financing is attractive to leverage into a larger deal.
- Upside potential. The property should have appreciation potential in the near future.

Unlike syndications and pensions funds, the entrepreneur varies much more in how the actual transaction is structured and the type of property sought.

In terms of financing, the entrepreneur may trade or leverage into larger properties. Typically, the entrepreneur seeks financing from the seller. Often, he will also seek secondary financing to shorten the gap between the first mortgage and the amount of cash risked.

The actual property could be anything — apartment buildings, retail neighborhood centers, smaller office buildings, business parks, old industrial buildings, or a vacant lot. The only requirement is that the property have upside potential.

The entrepreneur seeks to create value in the property that will lead to fast appreciation. Obsolete buildings can be retrofitted to meet market values. Entire properties can be developed. New tenants can be sought. The property can be managed more aggressively. Or value can be created by simply relandscaping or "dressing up" the property.

Here's a specific example of how an entrepreneur created value in a property and almost doubled his original investment in two years.

A 160,000-square-foot suburban office building was taken back in a mortgage foreclosure by a large institution. The institution managed the property for several years. Then, an entrepreneur saw that great value could be created in the property.

The entrepreneur needed only $2 million in cash to purchase the building with an existing first mortgage. After purchase, he created value in the property. First, he provided professional management for the property. He re-leased 30 percent of the space at substantially increased rentals and dressed up the property itself with new landscaping and a better general appearance.

Two years after the intitial investment, the entrepreneur sold a 65 percent interest in the property to an institutional investor for his original purchase price. He retained a 35 percent interest in the property. So, after two years, the entrepreneur essentially had gained a free interest in 35 percent of the property. That's making money. And fast!

Let's look at how another entrepreneur created value in a property and made money. It's also a good example of how the individual often can stick with a project that an institution could not.

Park Forest, Illinois was the first truly planned community in the United States. As part of that plan, a major regional shopping center was built 20 years ago.

Over time, the center deteriorated. The open-air design became obsolete. The tenant mix did not meet consumer needs. Vacancies occurred. And, as a result, the center had tremendous negative cash flows and the mortgage payments were not met. The property went into foreclosure.

An individual entrepreneur saw that the property had great redevelopment value. He obtained a first mortgage for the acquisition of the property with UDAC financing, a Federal program. Since this is a government type of financing, the individual needed considerable patience to obtain the grants.

Once the financing cleared, the entrepreneur razed a portion of the property, redesigned and enclosed the mall. During the reconstruction process, the entrepreneur managed to hold tenants and maintain a cash flow.

Turn-around time on the project was four years. At that time, the entrepreneur was able to sell a partial interest in the property for a good profit.

We can't emphasize enough that only an individual would have had the foresight and tenacity to carry out such a difficult transaction and redevelopment plan. And, that commitment really sums up how the successful entrepreneur buys real estate.

CORPORATE BUYERS

Corporations buy or build some of the most expensive real estate in the country. Often, the real estate they buy is more than a place to house their business; it also serves as a monument to their corporate identity. The Sears Tower is the largest office building in the world. Citicorp Plaza in New York City houses one of the largest banks in the world. The TransAmerica building in San Francisco is known worldwide for its distinguishable pinnacle.

The buying objectives of a corporation are usually straightforward:

- Primary use. The corporation wants a building that will house its operation.
- Identification. The corporation desires a symbol or image of itself as a corporate structure.
- Control. The corporation seeks to control the real estate it inhabits without restrictions that often come from landlords.
- Tax benefits. Ownership of real estate gives the corporation certain tax benefits.

While most large corporations purchase or develop property outright, smaller corporations can purchase real estate as well.

No matter what its size, a corporation that leases over one half of a building is often given the option to purchase the building at some time during the course of the lease agreement. For example, a company might occupy 300,000 square feet of a 600,000-square-foot office building. A 10 year lease usually would contain an option for the corporation to purchase the property. Or, if at some future date, the company occupied 75 percent of the property, a purchase option could be established.

The purchase option also protects the developer. When one tenant occupies more than 50 percent of one building, that tenant can put the project in jeopardy by moving. The purchase option allows the developer to protect the property and his interests.

A large corporate tenant also can get an equity option in a property that is vacant or under construction. This equity offer helps the developer attract large tenants as well as necessary financing.

Here's how we structured a real estate purchase for a corporation that met its buying objectives.

A major corporation signed a 10 year lease on 100 percent of the space in a new four-story building to serve as its worldwide headquarters. The company had the option to purchase the property up to 90 days after moving into the building. The company decided to purchase the building for several reasons.

First, the building provided good corporate identification for the company. It included an atrium that could be personalized by displaying all the important corporate symbols without objections from a landlord. Finally, ownership also gave the company control of maintenance and operation of the building, plus significant investment tax credits.

NEGOTIATING STRATEGIES AND TACTICS

Now that we've identified the major buyers of real estate, their objectives and the type of real estate they seek, we can turn to the actual purchase. It is during the actual purchase process that negotiating strategies and tactics come into play. Here are some examples:

Flexible Buying

One strategy involves accommodation on both the part of the buyer and the seller. Let's call it "flexible buying."

Buyer and seller — sitting across the table from each other — reach agreement on the price of a property. But, there's more to discuss than price. Form of payment must be negotiated. This may sound like a simple matter, but how the seller is paid can affect the price of the property.

For example, our seller and buyer agree to a price, but the seller wants payment over a long period of time secured by a first or second mortgage. This causes a higher or lower asking price for the property, depending on the interest rate desired by the seller.

Say the current market rate for interest is 10 percent and the seller needs a 12 percent rate over the term of the loan. To meet his objectives, the seller lowers the asking price of the property, taking back a higher rate of interest from the buyer over the term of the loan.

This works in reverse also — a higher price is paid for the property but at a lower interest rate. It should be noted that in either case, the price of the property is the same in real terms.

Accommodation is the key here. Both sides want to make the transaction happen and each works to satisfy the other's objectives.

In some cases, a seller gets a higher price for a property than its current market value by staying "flexible." A property may need upgrading and remarketing or releasing. The seller raises the price of the property to the level it would be after all the work is completed — a price the seller would not have been able to realize for a year or two.

When the seller takes this higher price, he obviously must give back something to the buyer. Usually, this "give back" is some type of unsecured or second mortgage financing.

One more example shows how the price of a property can be changed during negotiations. Many companies are driven to produce high earnings. Rather than receive all cash for a property and possibly take a loss, the company will demand a higher price for the property and offer some secondary lending in return. The seller records a nice profit, and the buyer gets his financing.

Again, the key is accommodation. Both parties want the deal. Each accommodates the other.

Static Buying and Selling

Sometimes a seller sets the price and terms for a property and will not negotiate. In a sense, this in itself is a negotiating strategy — waiting to get what he wants.

This "static" negotiation usually involves a corporate or institutional owner of real estate. After all, the institution has certain requirements and objectives and the financial muscle to wait until a buyer meets its objectives.

This puts the buyer in a vulnerable position. No matter what strategies and tactics the buyer suggests, the seller demands his original offer. And eventually, in most cases, the "static" seller of a good property gets what he wants. It's simply a matter of time.

Such a transaction occurred with a large insurance company and its suburban multi-tenant office building. The insurance company wanted to sell the property but set a certain price and demanded all cash.

A small syndication wanted to buy the building. The syndication was told that the insurance company's price and terms would have to be met. The syndication, instead, made four offers on the property in two weeks.

The first offer met the seller's price but involved a cash payment plus short-term financing. This offer was rejected. The syndication then offered a higher price and a longer financing period. This offer also was rejected.

Two more offers were made on the property before the buyer was convinced that he had to meet the seller's terms. Eventually, the buyer met the asking price and paid all cash for the property and arranged its own financing before the purchase.

A lesson learned!

Slow But Sure

An effective buying strategy that works many times could be called "slow but sure." Basically, the buyer finds a good property that the owner wants to sell. The buyer then prolongs negotiations, getting more and more concessions from the seller. At the same time, the seller becomes more and more anxious to sell, making it easier to grant concessions. This strategy is especially effective for older properties and properties not in high demand.

"Slow but sure" negotiations typically progress in the following manner. The buyer meets the price of the seller, but the sale is subject to certain conditions. These conditions vary from an engineering inspection to a review of the building's leases. The object of the conditions is to find a flaw in the property that will make the seller lower the price.

Let's look at some of the property conditions that should be evaluated in "slow but sure" negotiations.

The buyer should review the leases. If rents are fixed with options for rent renewal at the same rate, the buyer can claim the rents are under market. This will hold down the value of the property in years to come, thereby depreciating the overall value of the property.

A review of the leases also might show that operating costs and taxes are not passed through to the tenant. This decreases cash flow and therefore the value of the property.

In either case, the buyer asks for a price reduction.

The buyer should complete an engineering inspection of the property. Such an inspection might reveal equipment problems that could require a major capital improvement or cause a tenant to vacate. Equipment problems could include a poor ventilation system, antiquated elevators, or overloaded electrical devices — any major capital improvement needed to bring the building up to current operating standards.

Any of these conditions would decrease the value of the property. So, the buyer asks for a price reduction.

A review of financing on the property could reveal that the fixed rate mortgage is not assumable. Or, there may be a call provision in the mortgage demanding a review of interest rates every five or 10 years. This is the type of mortgage provision that commonly is not revealed in negotiations that will affect the value of the building. If such a provision is found, the buyer asks for a price reduction.

There are cases where this strategy is also successful for newer properties.

For example, there was a transaction where a foreign institution (an insurance company) wanted to buy a partial interest in four office buildings. Three had been recently completed and one was under construction. The properties were owned by an individual who was very anxious to sell a partial interest.

The buyer took the "slow but sure" approach (a fairly common approach with foreign buyers). Several months were spent drafting the complex legal documents for the sale, prolonging negotiations somewhat unnecessarily.

Meanwhile, the institution continued to seek other properties around the country. This "shopping" might lead to a better property and a better deal. "Slow but sure."

As time passed, the seller became more and more insistent on concluding the sale. Eventually, he conceded 85 percent of the tax benefits for the buyer's 65 percent interest in the property. A deal was struck — and quite a good one for the foreign institution.

Going slow can secure a better deal or a better property.

Getting Carried Away

Real estate, in some respects, is no different than buying an expensive car, a bottle of rare wine, or a piece of fine art. If someone's ego demands a property, he'll buy it no matter what the cost.

This is how some buyers — almost always individuals — get carried away. The situation is not always in the best economic interest of the buyer — but sellers love it. Individuals demanding a property can lead to bidding wars that increase the price of a property unnecessarily.

Recently, there was a case where an institution owned a newly completed suburban office building. The property had not finished leasing and "true value" had not yet been created.

An individual decided that he had to have the property. He made an all-cash offer of $2.5 million. The seller refused.

The buyer then offered $3.7 million and based on cash flows took a three percent yield. At this point, the seller had to sell. The institution knew that this kind of value could not be created even after the property was completely leased.

An individual's ego got carried away, and he paid more for the property than the economic value could justify.

The Fast Track

Everyone dreams of buying a property that is undervalued.

When a buyer does find an undervalued property, the key is to lock up the property as quickly as possible. Even standard conditions should be waived before the seller has the chance to realize that the property is worth far more than the asking price.

The astute buyer, keenly aware of market conditions, can use this technique effectively. It's surprising how often it works.

The owner of several buildings recently sold a buyer a good property. The owner suggested that the buyer consider another one of his buildings. After a quick look at the building, the buyer met the owner's asking price of $5 million. The buyer knew the property easily was worth $6 million or $7 million. It seems the seller had overlooked a clause in the lease that would raise rents substantially and increase the value of the property dramatically. In this case, the buyer had better market knowledge and a better understanding of certain lease provisions than did the owner of the building.

"Fast track" buying is especially common in land sales where the sellers of large land tracts typically are unsophisticated. The seller may not be aware that market rents in the area have risen causing a corresponding increase in the value of the raw land. For example, if rents in the area have risen from $15 to $17 per square foot, this could increase the land price of vacant land by 50 cents per square foot, making land worth millions of dollars more than before.

There is a variation on the "fast track." That's when the buyer locks up an undervalued property and then quickly resells it for a good profit.

The buyer signs a contract to purchase a property for $4 million with closing set in 90 days. The catch is that the property is clearly worth more than $4 million. Before closing, the buyer finds a second buyer willing to pay $5 million for the property. In 90 days, a simultaneous closing is held. First, the property is sold for $4 million. The buyer turns around immediately and resells the same property for $5 million. The first buyer gets a profit or "spread" of $1 million.

One More Example

There's one more example of negotiating the purchase of a property that shows just how complicated a commercial real estate transaction can be. It also demonstrates some of the principles we've talked about in this chapter.

It concerns a 40-story, 600,000-square-foot office building in Chicago's Loop. It was built in 1926. In 1965, about 75 percent of the building was retrofitted and air-conditioning was added.

The building had been fairly successful throughout the years. About half of the property was leased to one tenant and although rental rates were somewhat below market value, the building was 95 percent leased.

In 1972, a major corporation constructed a 1.5-million-square-foot office building just across the street, taking 600,000 square feet of that space. The corporation began to market the remainder of the space in direct competition with the "older" building. But the market was soft. Tenants were hard to attract.

After a year, the corporation decided to lease its building at any cost. They began leasing space well below market rates. As a result, numerous deals were lost to the corporation that would have been unprofitable for the "older" building over a 5 or 10 year lease period.

The owner of the "older" building, as an individual, realized he could not compete against the corporation and decided to sell. At first, he tried to sell the building to a real estate investment fund (REIT). These were corporate entities — popular in the 1970s — that could purchase real estate and pass on 90 percent of the cash flows to investors tax-free. Unfortunately, the owner found that the REIT funds wanted new properties or properties under construction.

Instead, an individual buyer was found.

The individual gave the owner $25,000 for a "30-day look" at the property. This deposit was non-refundable, giving him the contract to purchase the building.

The buyer then started his "slow but sure" negotiating tactics. The buyer put down another $25,000 every 30 days for the next three months, bringing his total to $100,000. During this time, he was trying to line up investors or financing and was also questioning the price and the value of the building.

Another six months passed and he put down another $150,000. At this point, the owner was getting more and more anxious to sell. The buyer also was determined that the corporation's building was a vital factor in the value of the property. Therefore, the price of the building was dropped by $200,000, setting the actual purchase price at $9.5 million.

While these negotiations were going on, a lease was being negotiated with the building's major tenant. But, the corporation landed the tenant for its building. When this happened, the negotiating process took an interesting turn. The buyer claimed a default on the original contract because the value of the building was lowered due to the loss of the major tenant. He demanded his money back.

After some tough negotiations, the price of the building was lowered by another $1 million. The buyer did not exonerate the seller of the technical default but did not actually claim a default either. The buyer then put up another $250,000, bringing his total deposit up to $500,000.

To complicate matters further, the mortgage market moved from seven to nine percent interest during the negotiation period. Market rental rates did not increase to offset these higher mortgage rates, thereby lowering the value of the property.

Three months later, the building was sold for $8.2 million. In total, it was 15 months of tough, complex negotiations.

This is a good example to show how complex and protracted negotiations can become when buying commercial real estate. The buyer used the "slow but sure" technique. The value of the property was affected by competition from another property. The climb in mortgage rates also lowered the value of the building. Finally, it's a good example of how an individual cannot compete with a larger corporation that is prepared to lease its property at any price and has the financial muscle to do so.

We hope that our examples have illustrated that the buyer's objectives determine the type of real estate that is sought and how it is finally purchased.

As we've seen, the buyer's objectives are not always logical ones. A large ego often drives the need for a certain property. But, in all cases, it is the initial objectives of the buyer that determines the outcome.

It is important to note that not all buyers of commercial real estate know the market. As we saw in some examples, buyers often make faulty buying decisions based on poor market knowledge or poor market assumptions.

Here, the experienced and knowledgeable broker provides invaluable assistance in identifying properties that truly meet the buyer's objectives. A broker also offers invaluable guidance during negotiations. Negotiations can be long and usually are tough. Since the broker negotiates these transactions on a daily basis, he has the experience to develop the best strategy.

As the market place evolves, the future of buying real estate as an investment promises on-going variety in the players and their relative importance.

Commercial real estate is one of several vehicles for the investment of money. In coming years, different investors will become the most active players depending on their objectives and the economic climate. At times, syndications will be most active. At other times, it could be pension funds or maybe foreign investors.

But, commercial real estate should always offer buyers tremendous tax benefits and a good hedge against inflation.

On the most basic level, we must never forget that real estate must compete with other financial vehicles — money market funds, stocks, bonds, gold, collectibles, and treasury bills. Money always demands the highest yields. So good buying decisions are a must. And, that's what makes buying real estate a great business challenge and also a great opportunity!

John Bruemmer, specializing in investment sales and office leasing, is senior vice-president of Royal LePage Commercial Real Estate Services, Inc.

Royal LePage is one of North America's largest diversified real estate organizations with offices in major U.S. and Canadian cities.

Ted Enloe

FINANCING COMMERCIAL REAL ESTATE PROJECTS

This chapter will provide a broad overview of the financing of commercial real estate projects. Six topics will be covered. First, an historical perspective examining the development of real estate finance in recent years will be established. Second, both historical and current sources of capital will be described. Next, common "structures" of commercial real estate financing arrangements will be discussed.

Other sections outline performance measures which are important in any financial arrangement and describe the role of mortgage bankers in the current marketplace. The chapter concludes with a discussion of the future of commercial real estate financing.

HISTORICAL PERSPECTIVE

Developers create value in a property by utilizing their skills to combine raw goods such as land, construction materials, and money into a building or development. A successful project creates synergies so that the value of the completed development is greater than the value of the individual components (land, bricks, mortar, steel, capital) of the structure. Although a property's financing is not as clearly identified with a building as its construction quality and its architectural design, financing has the potential to be either a property's greatest asset or its greatest liability.

Until the late 1970s and early 80s, virtually all commercial real estate financing carried fixed interest rates and offered amortization terms ranging from fifteen to forty years. America's post World War II economic boom and governmental policies created an environment which promoted increasingly liberal financing terms during the 1950s and 60s. The country's relatively stable economic environment helped make such long-term financing arrangements possible. Fixed-rate, long-term financing and economic conditions in the 1950s and 60s often allowed developers to "mortgage out"; that is, developers often were able to borrow 100% (sometimes more than 100%) of the cost of the project because the economic value created through the development process supported that level of financing.

Over a period of time, inflation caused long-term, fixed-rate financing to be a store of value for borrowers and an unprofitable endeavor for lenders. Initially, lenders were able to make an adequate spread between the interest they paid for use of funds and the money they earned on real estate loans. By the 1980s, deregulation of financial markets and inflation had created a situation in which most lenders' costs of funds were substantially above the yields being received on their outstanding loan portfolios. Inflation and expectations of future inflation led to the demise of the traditional fixed-rate mortgage.

In the 1970s, it had become practically impossible for developers to borrow 100% of the funds required for a project. Even when fixed-rate financing was available, higher interest rates and resulting higher income capitalization rates, coupled with a generally highly competitive real estate market, required developers to contribute increasing amounts of equity to projects. At the same time, however, lenders began to take equity positions in developments, hoping to increase their return on projects and provide a hedge against inflation. Today, it is common for lenders to receive a share of both current benefits and residual benefits (sales price and/or rental increases) of a property.

HISTORICAL SOURCES OF CAPITAL

Traditionally, entities which made loans on commercial real estate specialized in a particular area of real estate finance. Savings and loans held the majority of single-family home mortgages. Commercial banks were known primarily as sources for construction loans. Long-term financing for commercial real estate projects was dominated for years by life insurance companies.

For many years, life insurance companies had a stable source of funds because of the nature of product the companies handled. Premium income received and benefits distributed were largely predictable. This relatively stable source of funds made long-term investments feasible for life insurance companies. However, as inflation and inflation expectations increased, the nature of life insurance began to change. Whole life policies became less acceptable, and companies relied on term products or, more recently, universal life insurance as alternative instruments.

In the late 1970s and early 80s, policyholders in many life companies borrowed heavily against their existing policies. These policy loans were required to be made at substantially below-market interest rates. Like savings and loans, many life companies faced decreased profitability during this time period because of their obligations to provide previously contracted, low interest rate policy loans. In addition, new life insurance companies offered new life insurance products to consumers which took advantage of higher investment returns available in the marketplace and made it difficult for older mutual companies to compete with their older, lower-yielding portfolio of investments. Consequently, major life companies had fewer funds available to invest in real estate.

Mutual savings banks are financial intermediaries similar to savings and loans which are located primarily in northeastern states and in the state of Washington. Savings banks' commercial real estate lending consists primarily of loans for multi-family developments. These institutions face limitations on the type of loans and services they can offer simply because of the geographical separation between lenders and borrowers.

Pension funds did not begin to become a factor in commercial real estate finance until the early 1970s. The creation of the Prudential Property Investment Separate Account (PRISA) in 1970 is generally considered to be the point when pension funds began to view real estate as a feasible investment.

Commercial banks have historically concentrated on short-term lending in commercial real estate, primarily through construction lending. Banks obtain the majority of their funds through relatively short-term deposits. Thus, construction loans for terms of 12 to 24 months provide an optimal way for commercial banks to become involved in real estate finance.

Financial intermediaries such as General Electric Credit Corporation and other corporations known primarily for consumer finance also participate in commercial real estate lending. Like commercial banks, these firms are generally short-term lenders. Companies, like General Electric Credit Corporation are also known for offering standby commitments on construction loans. A standby commitment is a promise to fund a loan to retire the construction loan upon completion of construction; however, a standby commitment is most frequently issued in hopes that it will not be implemented and provides more onerous terms than permanent financing. The developer normally searches for permanent financing upon completion of the project and establishment of its economic value. A substantial commitment fee is charged by most companies which issue standby commitments.

For most of the 20th century, commercial real estate was financed with long-term, fixed rate mortgages. High inflation rates, changes in usury ceilings and deregulation of financial institutions caused drastic changes in financial markets during the late 1970s and early 1980s. The cost of funds for virtually all financial intermediaries rose considerably. To protect themselves from getting trapped into paying more for funds than their investments were yielding, lenders have taken steps in recent years to better match both the maturities of funding sources and investments and the spread between the cost of funds and investment yields.

CURRENT SOURCES OF CAPITAL

As alternatives to traditional fixed-rate lending have developed, sources of funds for commercial real estate development have also experienced significant changes. Pension funds were a relatively minor source of real estate finance as little as 15 years ago. Today, pension funds represent perhaps the fastest growing source of real estate finance funds in the nation.

By the end of 1982, the pension plans in the United States had investments in real estate which exceeded $20 billion and amounted to approximately 3% of total pension fund assets at that time. Pension fund investment in real estate has continued to grow; in fact, many experts forecast that funds will eventually invest as much as 15 to 20 percent of their total assets in real estate.

The limited historical data which is available on pension fund performance supports the theory that additional investment in real estate is a wise move. Between 1970 and 1982, PRISA consistently out-performed pension funds with primary investments in common stocks, long-term bonds and treasury bills.

Pension funds may be described as direct or indirect funds for investment purposes. A direct fund (generally a public pension fund) maintains its own staff which controls and administers the fund's investments. An indirect fund (generally a private pension fund) utilizes a financial intermediary such as a life insurance company, an investment banker, a bank, or a specially created management company to serve in an advisory capacity with respect to investments. Discretionary intermediaries are given authority to make decisions on investments, while non-discretionary intermediaries have limited decision-making power.

Companies serving as intermediaries for pension funds earn fees for originating, managing and liquidating investments. Fees are normally based on a percentage of the value of the assets being managed, or a percentage of the initial investment. Presently, life insurance companies are the most active intermediaries for pension funds. While life insurance companies had fewer funds available for investment during the early 1980s, they still retained large staffs of experts in the field of real estate finance. Many of these companies combined the expertise of their real estate department with money from pension funds to continue making commercial real estate investments.

Although life insurance companies today do not retain the role they played previously, these firms are still major players in real estate finance. Life insurance companies still finance some real estate with their own funds; however, most companies' general accounts funds are now put into inflation-hedged positions with terms generally shorter than ten years. Some life insurance companies are buying real estate for their own account, and many are undertaking joint ventures with developers who carry established track records.

A significant portion of life insurance companies' current involvement in real estate finance comes through negotiating Guaranteed Income Contracts (GIC) and managing investments for pension funds. A GIC is similar in nature to a certificate of deposit. GIC's are created when pension funds invest large amounts at fixed rates for a given number of years. Life insurance (life) companies guarantee the participating pension fund a certain return on its investment and then match the fund's investment with a corresponding loan on commercial real estate. These loans are made at an interest rate which provides the life company with a spread over its cost of funds under the GIC. The loans may be amortized over 20 to 30 years, but they are normally payable in full within 5 to 12 years, depending upon the length of time the pension fund wishes to have its money invested.

Savings banks and savings and loan associations nearly disappeared from real estate finance over the past few years because of the negative spread between their high cost of depository funds and their lower yields on investments. Savings banks have re-entered the real estate finance market, concentrating heavily on instruments which carry floating interest rates. Today's financing structures take on a variety of forms, but virtually all of them carry provisions for periodic renegotiation of terms or allow rates to be restated periodically depending on the level of a specified interest rate or index.

Foreign investors are becoming an increasingly large source of funds for real estate investment. Department of Commerce figures indicate that real estate surpassed manufacturing as the major area of foreign investment in the United States for the first time in 1981. Foreign investors are interested in real estate in the

United States for several reasons. First of all, the military and governmental system of the United States provides a degree of political stability which is not present in much of the rest of the world. Second, foreigners are often more aware of inflation than are Americans. Double-digit inflation can create near panic in the United States, yet many countries experience triple-digit inflation in a given year. Foreign investors believe that quality real estate provides an attractive hedge against inflation. A third reason foreigners invest in real estate in the United States is that cash yields offered on real estate investments in this country are typically more attractive than those offered elsewhere. Foreign investors are generally more interested in owning property in the United States than making loans to finance it. Although for tax reasons, their investment may sometimes be structured as a loan with an equity kicker. Levels of foreign investment are affected by factors such as the relative strength of the dollar against a given currency and the level of activity in Middle Eastern oil markets.

Over the past decade, syndication has become a major source of funds for commercial real estate projects. Syndications were originally created to meet the needs of developers for equity funds in a project and to provide affordable investments to relatively small investors seeking tax shelters. Syndications are conducted through public offerings or via private placement. Public offerings, generally vary substantially in size, are required to be registered with the Securities and Exchange Commission and are subject to numerous other governmental regulations. Syndications have raised enormous funds in recent years; however, the feasibility of investment in syndication for any individual is subject to fluctuation in tax laws.

The commercial banking industry has changed in recent years and banks have become more and more aggressive in real estate finance. Instead of offering strictly construction financing for short terms with take-out commitments from other institutions, many banks have moved into open-end construction loans or construction "mini-perms."

Real estate investment trusts — largely dormant from the mid-70s to 1980 — have begun to attract increasing amounts of funds for investment in real estate. These entities typically invest in commercial and multi-family rental projects and pass through to their investors 95% of their net income. Funds typically are raised from public and private offerings of shares or other securities. A number of trusts specialize their investments in certain types of projects — i.e., rental apartments, hotels — while others consider a variety of income-producing real estate projects. One trust —

Lomas and Nettleton Mortgage Investors — specializes in construction and development lending and competes with commercial banks in over 40 states for these investments.

STRUCTURE OF FINANCING

For decades, the structure of financing for most commercial properties was very similar. In today's market, however, it is virtually impossible to find two projects which have the same financial structures. Increased inflation expectations coupled with the lack of profitability experienced by lenders in real estate portfolios have given rise to many new forms of financing. Investors are requiring floating rates (sometimes with fixed pay rates and accrual of the balance) or offering fixed rates with an equity interest in the project.

Through participation mortgages, lenders may obtain a share of a development's net income and/or sales price without actually assuming a fee interest in the property. Income participation in a property may be based on a percentage of effective gross income or net income or a percentage of income above some specified minimum. Participation in reversion amounts on a property are normally based on net proceeds from sale (gross sales price less selling expenses and remaining mortagage balance).

Another approach to financing commercial real estate involves sale and subsequent leaseback of the land a development occupies. In such an arrangement, a lender earns an additional return through a groundlease. Land ownership gives a financing institution more control over a development than it would have in other financing arrangements. Sale and leaseback arrangements involving land allow the developer to retain depreciation benefits on structural improvements on the property. Important considerations in any type of sale/leaseback arrangement include terms of repurchase options or cancellation privileges which may be granted to the investor.

Several pension funds and life insurance companies have moved from strictly lending money on developments to purchasing properties for their own account. In fact, some of these companies have begun to create, design, and build their own developments. Properties which these traditional lenders purchase or build may be leveraged or unleveraged. Pension funds are primarily interested in purchasing debt-free properties, since tax regulations prevent them from utilizing benefits normally associated with leveraged real estate.

Still another popular vehicle for real estate finance is the joint venture between the developer and the financing source. In a joint venture, a financial institution may assume the role of an active partner in the development or remain a passive partner in a project. Joint venture structures normally give the financial partner greater control over the decision-making process in a development than would a participating mortgage.

Although developers give up a substantial interest in a property when the financial institution takes an equity interest in the property (whether by participating mortgage, sale/leaseback or other structure), such an arrangement carries benefits which may well be worth the share of the project which is relinquished. An equity participation structure generally allows a developer to raise all funds required for the project without additional equity capital. Under equity arrangements, financial institutions may not demand as stringent adherence to key ratios such as debt service coverage as would be required by traditional mortgage loans.

In today's real estate market, virtually every financial package for a development is unique. Combinations of the structures previously discussed can be tailored to a given project to meet objectives of developers and financial institutions. No particular structure can be termed "conventional" in today's market.

IMPORTANT ELEMENTS OF ANY FINANCING STRUCTURE

In any real estate transaction, it is important to be aware of some basic financial measures. All financing is based on projections of how much income a property will generate. Lenders normally demand an appraisal which indicates that a property is capable of producing a stable stream of income for a period of at least ten to fifteen years. Debt service coverage (net income divided by debt service) is a key concern for most lenders. Lenders want assurance that the property will at least produce enough income to service the debt it assumes, plus some margin to cushion against a downturn.

Another key consideration in real estate finance is the amount of tax leverage provided by the project. At times, financial structures may be arranged more for tax purposes than for economic reasons. Syndications have proven to be a successful tool for tapping equity capital markets largely due to the fact that they provide attractive income shelters and after-tax returns to individuals.

For years, the standard measure of return in real estate finance was the financing institutions's interest yield (including points) on its mortgage loan. In recent years, the turn to other financing structures and equity participations has caused more sophisticated techniques such as the internal rate of return on an investment to become the standard investment measure in the industry. A property's internal rate of return is simply the present value of the discounted cash flows it is expected to produce over the holding period an investor projects. The internal rate of return on an investment is a powerful tool for analysis; however, it is only as good as the assumptions which are used to calculate the measure. For this reason, many lenders still prefer to analyze properties on the basis of a cash-on-cash return. Cash-on-cash returns are both easier to project and to understand than are internal rates of return.

THE VITAL ROLE OF MORTGAGE BANKERS IN TODAY'S WORLD

In the rapidly changing world of commercial real estate finance, it is often difficult for individual financial institutions or developers to be constantly aware of what type of financing best suits their needs at a given moment and what competitive yields are available. Financing structures change frequently, and interest rates frequently fluctuate on a daily basis.

The major mortgage bankers are active in the market on a daily basis. They can provide a vital link between developers and financial institutions. Mortgage bankers deal with diverse types of projects, forms of financing, developers, financial institutions, and geographic markets, and they can be extremely useful in helping a developer or financial institution ascertain which arrangement best suits his needs. Entrepreneurial developers may lack the patience which is sometimes required to deal with large institutional lenders. Mortgage bankers may be able to bridge the "patience gap" for developers by working with established contacts in various institutions. In today's relatively complex financial environment, the services of a mortgage banker can be invaluable in shaping, structuring, and negotiating real estate transactions.

THE FUTURE OF COMMERCIAL REAL ESTATE FINANCE

Predicting the future of real estate finance is a bit like prognosticating the economy or declaring how large the federal deficit will be in a given future year. Ten years ago, it would have been difficult for even the most knowledgeable experts to project the changes which have occurred in the real estate finance industry since that time.

The future of real estate finance depends to a large degree on perceptions concerning inflation. Many lenders consider the long-term, fixed-rate mortgage to be an historical artifact; however, a sustained period of low inflation and economic stability could revive its use.

The real estate industry has become more and more institutionalized over the past decade. This trend can be expected to continue. Large financial institutions initially became involved in real estate purely as lenders. Next, they began to undertake joint ventures and issue participation mortgages. Now, companies frequently purchase and own the entire fee interest in projects, and some institutions actively participate in all phases of real estate development.

Even though large institutions control a tremendous amount of the capital available for real estate development and have the expertise to "invest" this capital successfully in projects, it is very much in question whether institutions can supplant the traditional entrepreneurial role of the developer. Questions abound as to the entrepreneurial talent and drive of these huge organizations and their ability to provide rewards to attract that caliber of talent.

In addition, many developers have grown to the point that they operate in many different markets and are, in fact, institutional in size and geographic penetration. However, their structure tends to be entrepreneurial and local market oriented as to decision-making and risk-taking. Certainly, the rewards are entrepreneurial.

The impact of the institutional developers tends to ebb and flow with the vagaries of the individuals within the organization. Age, varied interests, death, and the inevitable desire to "take it easy" or to "run your own show" result in spin-offs, break-ups, and withdrawals from markets and organizations.

Even though the trend to institutionalization will likely continue, there remains tremendous opportunity for the individual entrepreneur in real estate development. Real estate remains a local market. An individual with the ability to anticipate trends and needs, contract for land, secure zoning and governmental approvals, conceive and design the project, arrange financing, construct the project, and market and lease and/or sell the project will still be in great demand.

Ted Enloe is the president of Lomas & Nettleton Financial Corporation, America's largest mortgage banking firm. Mr. Enloe is also president of Lomas & Nettleton Mortgage Investors and L&N Housing Corporation. Mr. Enloe is a director of the Federal Reserve Bank of Dallas. He is a director of the Dallas Development Corporation and the Dallas Chamber of Commerce, and has served as director of the Metropolitan United Way and governor for the National Association of Real Estate Investment Trusts.

C. E. "Doc" Cornutt

THE COST TO BUILD

We are reminded of the recurring quote from the president of a large construction company speaking to his developer clients:

"There are only two exciting times in any real estate project — the first is when you start, the second is when you finish, and everything in between is just plain hard work."

Although it is fun to write about groundbreakings where new shovels take their first scoop of dirt or ribbon cuttings where a project looks brand spanking new, this chapter deals with some of the critical elements to a project's success that fall in the "everything-in-between" stage. The cost to build any project stays on the developer's mind throughout the project since ultimately it becomes the investment base upon which future returns will be judged. As real estate developers who have watched some of the largest in the country who make their home in Dallas — namely Trammell Crow, Mac Pogue and John Eulich — just to mention a few, we are convinced that successful developers are those active "hands-on" types who have a specific development strategy in mind and implement it. Consequently, the *cost to build* is not just focusing on the *dollars*, but most important of all, the "*sense*" that permeates the project from Day One.

In the past ten years, inflation has bailed out many projects which were over budget when constructed, inadequately financed, or did not meet rent proformas when initially complete. As we all look back to the good old days, we must remind ourselves that the marketplace and economic environment are much different today. Long term lenders and financial institutions have different requirements today than they did in years past. Now they want shorter loans, less risk, more coverage, and a higher yield than developers gave them in the 60s and 70s. Furthermore, competition in the marketplace for developers today has increased significantly. There are many more players on the field in all development areas — commercial, office, industrial, apartment, and residential — and this rivalry has forced every developer to look closely at:

- The product that is to be built
- The market share that can be obtained
- The financing that can be put in place
  — *before ever arriving at what it costs to build.*

These market and financing factors, along with a developer's economic return requirements, dictate what completing a project will cost the developer. Today, with interest rates much higher than developers want to pay and operating deficits during lease up periods a much bigger factor, it becomes extremely important to provide adequate focus on the *cost to build* any project — not just the numbers, but everything that goes on behind those numbers.

The success (or lack thereof) of any project is due in large part to how it is addressed before the construction process is ever commenced. A project's financial and developmental success will be decided by the marketplace and the economic return that is achieved. This chapter will address the key areas that must be considered if the project is to be completed within budget, on schedule, and within desired quality standards. These elements are:

- Project Description
- Project Team
- Project Schedule
- Project Budget and Proformas
- Project Organization

PROJECT DESCRIPTION

Every real estate project starts with a "spark" that gleams in a developer's eyes. It reflects the concept which could ultimately become reality. We're sure that far more real estate projects have been conceived on a paper napkin than in the corporate board rooms of America. Real estate development is entrepreneurial in every sense of the word. History has proven in the real estate business that timing and quick reactions and decisions have produced leased up buildings while those who hesitated got caught in the "overhang" between tight and surplus markets. We recall the investment advice that, "An investor is one who gambles and wins while a speculator is one who gambles and loses."

Yet, today's environment and "cash flow" pressures force those who want to be successful developers to take a project to a point where it is a "gut cinch" or more importantly (in tough times at least), where he can "walk" the deal, or defer the start of the project until it is economically more feasible. Most project financings today are nonrecourse in name only, and with a developer's name always being on the line, this front end planning process is critical.

The money spent putting a Project Description together with a Project Team is probably the best money infused into the project. In our $250,000,000 of project experience, we have yet to see any project that did not have several stumbling blocks to overcome before the bulldozers circled the block. Only the front end seed money identified how these problems could best be solved.

The importance of preparing a detailed development program is essential to properly outlining the project scope and anticipated costs by categories. The Project Description should include descriptions of:

- Property acquisition (if not already owned)
- Overall project narrative and summary of facts
- Site plan
- Facilities Summary (backed up by building elevations, sections, floor plans, and area tabulations)
- Key market demand and marketing factors
- Outline construction specifications

A seed money budget should be established to take the project to a go-no-go decision point, including:
- Design schematics and related engineering
- Marketing materials (models, audio visual, etc.) to determine project acceptance and firm up lease commitments
- Economic and budget analysis including project appraisal work

PROJECT TEAM

When it comes to recommending how much or to what extent a Project Team is put together, we find ourselves recalling the story of *Goldilocks and the Three Bears*. Each developer must individually taste the soup, sit in the chair and lie down on the bed to determine what is "just right" when it comes to assembling the Project Team. We have seen numerous instances across the country where projects were delayed or experienced budget problems because specialized consulting (such as acoustical engineering or traffic engineering, for example) were not commissioned by the developers in the project's early stages. Furthermore, with the break up of AT&T in 1984 and the resulting changes and corporate requirements that have occurred in the telecommunications industry, we recognize that a telecommunications consultant is much more necessary today in this area. Ten years ago, all you had to do was call the phone company.

Here is a list of possible consulting needs for the Project Team. Each of these disciplines needs consideration and many require the employment of a specialized consultant.

Design
- Architectural
- Mechanical and Electrical Engineering
- Structural Engineering
- Interior Design/Space Planning
- Landscape Architectural
- Lighting
- Geotechnical Engineering
- Vertical Transportation
- Civil Engineering
- Traffic
- Surveying
- Acoustics
- Food Service
- Energy Management
- Security
- Telecommunications

Construction
- General Construction
- Mechanical/Electrical Construction
- Exterior Facade
- Vertical Transportation
- Structural Systems
- Testing

Development
- Auditing
- Legal Counsel
- Financing
- Insurance
- Property Management
- Advertising/Public Relations
- Purchasing

The selection process of Project Team members should be well thought out since this is the group that really runs the show. All Project Team members should be closely examined in terms of:

- Prior projects and work experience
- Size, existing work load, and the ability to meet deadlines

- Financial stability (or potential lack thereof, if the bottom should fall out of the economy)
- Depth of competent staff
- Chemistry with the other members of the Project Team and commitment by principals (firm owners) to the project being undertaken

We can't overemphasize the importance of each firm's *commitment* to perform. An important project to one group may not be of the same importance to another. Make sure you see that "hungry look" and all the excitement to perform for you, the developer client. Also, make sure that the Project Team stays a team because chemistry and balance are important.

Many of the successful relationships between design consultants, construction trades, and development professionals already exist. When developing the $75,000,000 Hyatt Regency Dallas and Reunion Tower, our firm had the explicit rule that we would not consider utilizing any company that had not been involved in at least three projects of comparable magnitude. This turned out to be cheap insurance to complete the project in budget and on schedule.

There are several key issues affecting the project in the earliest development stage which reinforces the need for a complete Project Team.

All factors affecting the municipal role and relationship must be fully understood and outlined, such as:

- Street system
- Utilities, abandonment or relocation
- Existing easements
- Infrastructure cost allocation
- Building codes and zoning ordinances/variances
- Parking/traffic requirements

We can still recall hearing the stories about several projects which the completed building encroached on the adjoining property because of a property discrepancy left unresolved.

If historic preservation is involved, a detailed status should be made of the proposed project as it relates to:

- Tax incentive programs
- Involvement/role of local historical group(s)
- Historic preservation certification for development plans
- Inspection/documentation

Historical renovation can be summarized by the colorful, and only somewhat exaggerated quote, attributed to Trammell Crow, that "historic renovation work should be bid out to three separate contractors and the final cost to the owner will be the sum total of those three bids." Our firm has probably done the largest historic renovations in the Dallas-Fort Worth area. We can't think of any other type of project that could be more rewarding (converting the old to the new) and satisfying (the revitalization of the center city). Just make sure you are approaching it with the "used car" theory in mind — you don't know what's under the hood.

The construction team's input should be brought into the project at the earliest possible stage to provide preliminary insight into:

- Project Schedule and Budget
- Key delivery factors: steel, elevators, labor contract expiration dates, weather cycles
- Key building components and techniques (concrete vs. steel, exterior facade type, etc.)
- Electrical service
- Infrastructure problems
- Construction mobilization and flow
- Break out of components between base contract (general contractor) and other trades (tenant finish)
- Fast track versus design/bid decision

Once the design is complete, the project comes down to being built and the same problems and questions come up over and over again. The contractor (as long as he does not aspire to do architectural. design) can provide input that can streamline the design process and provide guidance on setting the Project Schedule and Budget. The Contractor can also help establish key design/construction decisions and the target dates to achieve them. Some developers have their own in-house construction management staff providing this construction expertise. Most contractors, in our experience, will provide assistance to the Project Team during the schematic design phase since it, in essence, puts them at an advantage of knowing the project fully when bidding time comes around.

In summary, if the development project is to be fully designed and outlined to a point where the economic package (budget and proformas), financing (interim and permanent), and market response are signed off by the owners/developer — then the Project Team must be assembled and a significant seed money budget must be established. The greater the seed money budget, the more exposure is reduced. Most of the consulting professionals will perform initially on a cost reimbursement basis and will take their profit later by betting on the developer.

PROJECT SCHEDULE

If the Project Team collectively establishes an overall Project Schedule (which can be updated periodically), then the major milestone dates surface along with the detail benchmark dates in between. This development and construction management tool can help assure the project is completed on time and in budget. There are several givens when it comes to scheduling.

Any day lost at the beginning of the project will probably cost you two days at the end of the project. Many times the production of working drawings can be delayed because of lack of information or approvals, etc. Without proper coordination and the team working together, it becomes like the 440 yard relay when the timing is bad and the runner's baton is dropped. Everyone expects the contractor to make up any time delays which originated prior to the start of construction. It simply cannot work that way.

If you want to adhere to the schedule, then make sure the project is organized to handle the decision and problem solving process. All fingers point back to the owner no matter what goes wrong. Also make sure everyone remembers the critical dates — even if it means tattooing them on everyone's arm. On our one-million-square-foot, 40-story Continental Plaza office building in Fort Worth, we sent out rulers during construction to the Project Team that had the calendar of critical completion dates notated as a reminder for them. Furthermore, at the end of every project, our firm has made it a practice of having a formal completion party. All the members of the Project Team attend with their spouses and celebrate (at the owner's expense, of course!) the project's substantial completion. These dollars are really insignificant when compared to the daily interest costs if the project is slow in finishing.

Don't forget that the squeaking wheel is the one that gets the grease.

A demanding "hands-on" developer can help assure that the schedule is followed. The job for the Project Team is a lot more fun, (and definitely more profitable), because the work for both consultant and contractor can be scheduled to avoid start/stop problems.

The successful developer should also make some due diligence trips to other comparable completed projects to not only obtain a perspective of the way the project was schedule and flowed, but also to look at:

- Design and budget considerations
- Back of house support and layout
- New systems (e.g., energy management, telecommunications)
- What went right?
- What went wrong?
- What work was cut from the original budget and was subsequently added back to the job?

Remember, we're all trying to build a better mousetrap, so take a look at somebody else's every once in a while.

On major high-rise or mixed-use projects, make sure that the contractor selected for the Project Team has the scheduling sophistication to assure the project's completion on time. We always wondered about the need for critical path schedules until we saw several projects (our competitors, of course!) where the whole job site was brought to a standstill because the job sequence was not properly identified and laid out.

Since the construction cost of any project is the largest single element, it becomes extremely important not only to complete the general construction within budget, but also to understand when the construction dollars will be spent. A good development economic model must take construction period interest and project what could occur under different time schedules, monthly draw-down rates, and interest ranges. But remember, the interest rate the last half of the project is far more important than the one on the first half. It is a certainty that a project can be over budget if the schedule is delayed or premium overtime is spent to bring it back on schedule.

Don't forget who you're turning the building over to as the Project Schedule is being prepared. If the building is a hotel, make sure the operator fully outlines all of the pre-opening requirements (telephone, building offices, storage space, etc.) If the building is an office building, have the property management team identify their space needs and turnover schedule to satisfy the tenant commitments. Sometimes construction dust and hard hats work against the operations people, unless they help build the Project Schedule. We can project three events that will occur with predictable regularity unless the project is scheduled right:

1. Building areas that the permanent operating staff need early will wind up being that space which the contractor is unable to com-

plete and turn over early. (By luck, this always turns out to be the contractor's on-site offices!)

2. The building's central plant will not be ready when the operations engineers are ready to take it over. (The central plant usually is ready to be tested one week before the key on-site mechanical and electrical people have received notices from their management that they need to move on to another project!)

3. Telephone service for operations will always be requested sooner than anyone ever anticipated.

If the total Project team is consulted on the Project Schedule at the outset, the project stands a fighting chance of making it, at least in today's times.

PROJECT BUDGET AND PRO FORMAS

After the Project Team has completed the Project Description, under the developer's direction, the numbers must be put together for the Project Budget and Pro formas. The financing stage of the project and strategy that goes along with it are totally based on the scope of the project and what the financial indicators say. In this section, we will briefly address budgets and pro formas since the rest of the chapter determines what information goes into them.

The major components of most Project Budgets are:

- General Conditions, contractor's fee, contractor's contingency, owner
  furnished construction materials/services
- Site work/utilities
- Exterior and interior landscaping
- Architectural and engineering fees
- Surveys, permits, testing
- Owner's insurance premiums (during construction)
- Real estate taxes (during construction)
- Interim interest
- Brokerage fee for financing and commitment fee
- Legal fees
- Preopening expenses (property management)
- Land cost (and building cost if a restoration/rehabilitation project)
- Furniture, fixtures and equipment (FF&E)
- Developer overhead
- Owner's construction contingency (increased during project by projected construction savings)
- Operating deficits to break even

Once you have the budget outlined, proformas must be prepared to determine the return on investment capabilities of the project. Here are a few thoughts about proformas:

- Make sure your computer model has the sophistication to generate all of the variations of the project's financing possibilities and phasing. You must be able to plug in new rates and variables and immediately know what the impact is. Most of the computer software packages now have the work sheet capacities to program and assemble multiple amounts of detailed information.
- Pro formas are worthless without the detailed market analysis of the competition — both primary and secondary. The use of an economic feasibility/market analysis consultant is often recommended and many times required by the lender. The Pro formas should obviously tell the lender that the project is feasible and has merit; but more importantly, it should confirm the viability of the project and the marketplace.
- Distinguish the Pro formas between the lease up period and stabilized operations. Most projects started in the late 70s still have not performed according to the projections prepared with a "compounded percentage increase per year" mentality.
- Fully explain all tax benefit considerations in the Pro formas. Make sure the Pro formas are up-to-date on all tax aspects.
- Spend some money putting together a polished mortgage package. We are amused at some of the names developers use to refer to the mortgage package. Our firm calls it the "Silver Bullet." Lincoln Property calls it the "Smoker." The renderings, site plans, layouts and all other descriptions must tell the project's complete story when reviewed 1000 miles away. Most lenders can quickly review the mortgage package and tell you if you have a "slam dunk."

The following exhibits represent standard Budget and Pro forma formats for hotels, office buildings, apartments, retail centers, and industrial parks.

This information is offered to represent format and the individual cost components. Obviously, the actual costs will fluctuate over time because of land prices and construction costs including interest.

OFFICE BUILDING — 208,500 SQUARE FEET
REPRESENTATIVE PROJECT BUDGET

Account Description	*Budget*
Land and Related	
Land Cost	$1,648,529
Real Estate Taxes	15,000
SUB TOTAL	1,663,529
Shell and Related	
Architectural and Engineering	
Survey and Platting	10,000
Soils Analysis	25,000
Landscape Architect	26,000
Architect and Engineering Fees	300,000
Reproduction	25,000
Architect Lender Inspection	15,000
Civil Engineers Fee	30,000
Elevator Consultant	5,000
Schedule Consultant	35,000
Graphics Consultant	15,000
Fountain Consultant	5,000
Builder's Risk Insurance	11,000
Building Permits	200,000
Contingency	500,000
General Conditions & Construction	7,700,000
Landscaping	270,000
Security	5,000
Signage and Graphics	50,000
Testing and Inspection	30,000
SUB TOTAL	9,257,000
Tenant Improvement/Construction	
Leasing Agent Commissions	241,250
Tenant Improvements	1,264,500
SUB TOTAL	1,505,750
Administration and Overhead	350,000
Advertising and Promotion	350,000
Closing and Title Fees	145,000
Construction Period Interest	740,000
Lease-Up Deficit/Interest Expense	658,721
Leasing Salary and Proposal Expense	60,000
Legal/General/Miscellaneous	60,000
Loan/Finance Fees	160,000
Tenant Inducements	100,000
SUB TOTAL	2,623,721
PROJECT TOTAL	$15,050,000

OFFICE BUILDING
REPRESENTATIVE PROJECT PRO FORMAS

	Quarter 2 1985	Quarter 3 1985	Quarter 4 1985
ASSUMPTIONS			
Rentable Square Footage (RSF)	92,642	93,642	93,642
Parking Spaces	84	84	84
Lease-Up Assumptions			
% Absorbed-Quarterly	30		
% Absorbed-Cumulative	30	20	
		50	20
			70
Office Rent/RSF-Spec	20.00	20.00	20.00
Parking Rate/Space*	1200	1200	1200
Escalation Rate-Rent (Spec)	0.00	0.00	0.00
Escalation Rate-Parking	0.00	0.00	0.00
Escalation Rate-Expenses	0.00	0.00	0.00
Total RSF Occupied	28,093	46,821	65,549
Total Parking Occupied	84	84	84
Expenses per RSF			
Cleaning	0.42	0.42	0.42
Electrical Supplies	0.02	0.02	0.02
HVAC	0.02	0.02	0.02
Elevator Maintenance	0.21	0.21	0.21
General Building Expense	0.55	0.55	0.55
Security	0.57	0.57	0.57
Administrative	0.70	0.70	0.70
Energy (Net)	0.08	0.08	0.08
Insurance	0.06	0.06	0.06
Taxes (County)	0.19	0.19	0.19
Taxes (City/School)	0.53	0.53	0.53
Management Fee	0.21	0.33	0.45
Total Expenses	3.56	3.68	3.80
TOTAL CAPITAL	12,250,000	12,250,000	12,250,000
CONVENTIONAL DEBT	$12,250,000	$12,250,000	$12,250,000
DEBT CONSTANT**	.13	.13	.13

* Assumes monthly rate of $75 per space adjusted to reflect after hours parking.
** 13.00%; 10 years interest only; 10 year maturity.

Quarter 1 1986	Quarter 2 1986	Quarter 3 1986	Quarter 4 1986
93,642	93,642	93,642	93,642
84	84	84	84
20	5	0	0
90	95	95	95
21.00	21.00	21.00	21.00
1260	1260	1260	1260
0.05	0.00	0.00	0.00
0.05	0.00	0.00	0.00
0.05	0.00	0.00	0.00
84,278	88,960	88,960	88,960
84	84	84	84
0.44	0.44	0.44	0.44
0.02	0.02	0.02	0.02
0.02	0.02	0.02	0.02
0.22	0.22	0.22	0.22
0.58	0.58	0.58	0.58
0.60	0.60	0.60	0.60
0.74	0.74	0.74	0.74
0.08	0.08	0.08	0.08
0.06	0.06	0.06	0.06
0.19	0.19	0.19	0.19
0.80	0.80	0.80	0.80
0.60	0.63	0.63	0.63
4.35	4.38	4.38	4.38
12,250,000	12,250,000	12,250,000	12,250,000
$12,250,000	$12,250,000	$12,250,000	$12,250,000
.13	.13	.13	.13

OFFICE BUILDING
REPRESENTATIVE PROJECT PRO FORMAS

OPERATIONS	Quarter 2 1985	Quarter 3 1985	Quarter 4 1985
Revenues			
Office Rental Revenues	140,463	234,105	327,747
Parking Revenues	25,200	25,200	25,200
Gross Revenues	165,663	259,305	352,947
Operating Expenses			
Cleaning	9,832	9,832	9,832
Electrical Supplies	468	468	468
HVAC	468	468	468
Elevator Maintenance	4,916	4,916	4,916
General Building Expense	12,876	12,876	12,876
Security	13,344	13,344	13,344
Administrative	16,387	16,387	16,387
Energy (Net)	1,873	1,873	1,873
Insurance	1,405	1,405	1,405
Taxes (County)	4,448	4,448	4,448
Taxes (City/School)	12,408	12,408	12,408
Management Fee	4,970	7,779	10,588
Total Expenses	83,395	86,204	89,013
Net Operating Income	82,268	173,101	263,933
Debt Service			
Conventional Debt	398,125	398,125	398,125
Other Debt	0	0	0
Subtotal, Debt Service	398,125	398,125	398,125
NET CASH FLOW	-315,857	-225,024	-134,192

Quarter 1 1986	Quarter 2 1986	Quarter 3 1986	Quarter 4 1986
442,458	467,039	467,039	467,039
26,460	26,460	26,460	26,460
468,918	493.499	493.499	493,499
10,324	10,324	10,324	10,324
492	492	492	492
492	492	492	492
5,162	5,162	5,162	5,162
13,520	13,520	13,520	13,520
14,011	14,011	14,011	14,011
17,207	17,207	17,207	17,207
1,966	1,966	1,966	1,966
1,475	1,475	1,475	1,475
4,448	4,448	4,448	4,448
18,728	18,728	18,728	18,728
14,068	14,805	14,805	14,805
101.892	102.630	102,630	102,630
367,026	390,870	390,870	390,870
398,125	398,125	398,125	398,125
0	0	0	0
398,125	398,125	398,125	398,125
-31.099	-7.255	-7.255	-7.255

OFFICE BUILDING
REPRESENTATIVE PROJECT PRO FORMAS

STABILIZED OPERATIONS	1987	1988	1989	1990
Revenues				
Office Rental Revenues	$1,961,566	$2,059,644	$2,162,626	$2,270,75
Parking Revenues	111,132	116,689	122,523	128,64
Gross Revenues	2,072,698	2,176,333	2,285,149	2,399,40
Operating Expenses				
Cleaning	43,361	45,529	47,805	50,19
Electrical Supplies	2,065	2,168	2,276	2,39
HVAC	2,065	2,168	2,276	2,39
Elevator Maintenance	21,680	22,764	23,903	25,09
General Building Expense	56,782	59,621	62,602	65,73
Security	58,847	61,789	64,879	68,12
Administrative	72,268	75,882	79,676	83,65
Energy (Net)	8,259	8,672	9,106	9,56
Insurance	6,194	6,504	6,829	7,17
Taxes (County)	17,792	17,792	17,792	17,79
Taxes (City/School)	78,659	82,592	86,722	91,05
Management Fee	59,220	65,290	68,554	71,98
Total Expenses	427,193	450,771	472,420	495,15
Net Operating Income	1,645,505	1,725,562	1,812,728	1,904,2:
Debt Service	1,592,500	1,592,500	1,592,500	1,592,50
NET CASH FLOW	$ 53,005	$ 133,062	$ 220,228	$ 311,7

Notes:
Revenue Escalation Assumption: 5.00%
Expense Escalation Assumption: 5.00%
Debt Service Constant: .13 (13.00%; interest only; 10 year)

1991	1992	1993	1994	1995	1996
$2,384,295	$2,503,510	$2,628,686	$2,760,120	$2,898,126	$3,043,032
135,082	141,836	148,928	156,374	164,193	172,402
2,519,377	2,645,346	2,777,614	2,916,494	3,062,319	3,215,434
52,705	55,341	58,108	61,013	64,064	67,267
2,510	2,635	2,767	2,905	3,051	3,203
2,510	2,635	2,767	2,905	3,051	3,203
26,353	27,670	29,054	30,507	32,032	33,634
69,019	72,470	76,094	79,898	83,893	88,088
71,529	75,105	78,861	82,804	86,944	91,291
87,842	92,235	96,846	101,689	106,773	112,112
10,039	10,541	11,068	11,622	12,203	12,813
7,529	7,906	8,301	8,716	9,152	9,610
17,792	17,792	56,212	72,470	76,094	79,898
95,611	100,391	105,411	110,682	116,216	122,026
75,581	79,360	83,328	87,495	91,870	96,463
519,020	544,081	608,817	652,706	685,343	719,608
2,000,356	2,101,264	2,168,796	2,263,789	2,376,978	2,495,827
1,592,500	1,592,500	1,592,500	1,592,500	1,592,500	1,592,500
$ 407,856	$ 508,764	$ 576,296	$ 671,289	$ 784,478	$ 903,327

HOTEL COMPLEX
OUTLINE OF REPRESENTATIVE PROJECT BUDGET

NOTE: Since hotels can vary widely because of size, location and density, there are no general cost rules for all projects. The budget outline below should give a representative sample of construction costs to be considered.

1. LAND
   Land Costs
   Land Acquisition Loan Interest
   Escrow Fee
   Closing Costs
   Land Legal Fee
   Brokers Fee
   Appraisal Fee
   Survey
   Title Policy
   Zoning Fee
   Ad Valorem Taxes Until Construction
   Maintenance Until Construction
   Land Letter of Credit Fee
   Off-site Improvements

2. FINANCING BEFORE CONSTRUCTION
   Market Studies
   Loan Submission Costs
   Financing Legal Fee
   Construction Lender Legal Fee
   Construction Loan Fee
   Permanent Lender Legal Fee
   Permanent Loan Fee
   Letter of Credit Fee

3. FINANCING DURING CONSTRUCTION
   Ad Valorem Taxes
   Construction Period Interest
   Construction Loan Income
   Construction Lender Inspection Fee
   Permanent Loan Interest
   Permanent Loan Income
   Permanent Lender Inspection Fee

4. PROFESSIONAL CONSULTANTS
   Architect Fee
   Structural Engineer Fee
   Mechanical Engineer Fee
   Electrical Engineer Fee
   Civil Engineer Fee

Soil Testing Engineering Fee
Landscape Architect Fee
Land Planner Fee
Traffic Engineer Fee
Interior Designer Fee
Lighting Designer Fee
Graphic Designer Fee
Kitchen Designer Fee
Laundry Designer Fee
Acoustical Engineer Fee
Sound System Designer Fee
Phone System Designer Fee
Communications Engineer Fee
Energy Management Designer Fee
Property Management Designer Fee
Operations Designer Fee
Life Safety Engineer Fee
Materials Testing Engineer Fee
Design Review Engineer Fee
Construction Estimator Fee
Elevator Engineer Fee
Construction Manager Fee
Scheduling Consultant Fee
Artist Fee
Consultants Reimbursables

5. OWNER CONTROLLED CONSTRUCTION
Demolition
Contract Legal Fee
Design, Printing and Models
Design Mock-ups
Additional E&O Insurance
Building Permits
Utility Connection Fees
OCIP Premiums
Builders Risk Premium
Construction Site Office
Project Signs
Progress Photos
Exterior Graphics
Interior Graphics
Kitchen Equipment
Laundry Equipment
Trash Equipment
Interior Finish Construction

6. CONSTRUCTION
General Conditions
Site Work
Concrete
Masonry
Metals
Carpentry
Moisture Protection
Doors, Windows and Glass
Finishes
Specialties
Equipment
Furnishings
Special Construction
Conveying Systems
Mechanical
Electrical
Bonds
Retainage
General Contractors Fee
Landscaping
Renovation to Existing Building
Other Miscellaneous
Contingency

7. FURNITURE FIXTURES AND EQUIPMENT
Guest Spaces
Public Spaces
Operating Equipment
Expendables
Handling and Warehousing
Special Systems

8. OPERATIONS
Pre-opening
Leasing
Working Capital and Operating Inventory
Operating Deficits

9. GENERAL AND ADMINISTRATIVE
Travel
Development Fee
Accounting and Audit Fees
Utilities During Construction
Advertising and Public Relations
Staff Relocation Costs
Investment Tax Credit Review
Contingency

HOTEL COMPLEX
REPRESENTATIVE PROJECT PRO FORMAS

OPERATING RATIOS

(Opening Date: June 1987)	1987	1988	1989	1990
Projected Occupancy	60%	65%	70%	70%
Revenues:				
Rooms Department	51.4%	51.6%	51.8%	51.8%
Food and Beverage Department	45.0	44.8	44.6	44.6
Telephone Department	2.6	2.6	2.6	2.6
Other Income	1.0	1.0	1.0	1.0
TOTAL REVENUES	100.0	100.0	100.0	100.0
Less				
Department Costs and Expenses:				
Rooms Department	11.6	11.4	11.3	11.3
Food and Beverage Department	34.4	33.8	33.2	33.2
Telephone Department	2.2	2.2	2.2	2.2
Total Department Costs and Expenses	48.3	47.5	46.7	46.7
TOTAL OPERATING DEPARTMENT INCOME	51.7	52.5	53.3	53.3
Less				
Undistributed Costs and Expenses				
Administrative and General	7.6	7.3	7.0	7.0
Marketing	4.4	4.2	4.0	4.0
Operation and Maintenance	4.9	4.6	4.4	4.4
Energy Costs	4.5	4.4	4.3	4.3
Total Undistributed Costs and Expenses	21.4	20.6	19.8	19.8
INCOME BEFORE FIXED CHARGES	30.3	32.0	33.5	33.5
Less				
Fixed Charges:	4.0	4.1	4.3	4.7
INCOME BEFORE MANAGEMENT FEES	26.4	27.8	29.1	28.7
Less				
Management Fees	3.0	3.0	3.0	3.0
INCOME BEFORE DEBT SERVICE	23.4	24.8	26.1	25.7
ROOMS DEPARTMENT PROFIT MARGIN	77.4	77.8	78.3	78.3
FOOD AND BEVERAGE DEPARTMENT PROFIT MARGIN	23.5	24.5	25.4	25.4
FOOD AND BEVERAGE ROOMS RATIO	87.6	86.8	86.0	86.0

HOTEL COMPLEX
REPRESENTATIVE PROJECT PRO FORMAS

CONSOLIDATED INCOME STATEMENT

(Opening Date: June 1987)	1987	1988	1989	1990
Project Occupancy	60%	65%	70%	70%
Revenues:				
Rooms Department	$ 3,293,400	$ 6,408,500	$ 7,322,000	$ 7,773,600
Food and Beverage Department	2,886,000	5,561,700	6,294,600	6,682,900
Telephone Department	164,700	320,400	366,100	388,700
Other Income	66,600	128,900	146,400	155,500
TOTAL REVENUES	6,410,700	12,419,500	14,129,100	15,000,700
Less				
Department Costs and Expenses:				
Rooms Department	745,200	1,419,900	1,589,600	1,687,600
Food and Beverage Department	2,206,600	4,199,900	4,696,500	4,986,000
Telephone Department	143,900	276,100	311,200	330,400
Total Department				
Costs and Expenses	3,095,700	5,895,900	6,597,300	7,004,000
TOTAL OPERATING DEPARTMENT				
INCOME	3,315,000	6,523,600	7,531,800	7,996,700
Less				
Undistributed Costs and Expenses:				
Administrative and General	487,900	907,000	993,100	1,054,200
Marketing	282,800	523,600	570,800	606,100
Operational and Maintenance	311,000	576,200	628,500	667,000
Energy Costs	288,300	547,800	611,400	649,100
Total Undistributed				
Costs and Expenses	1,370,000	2,554,600	2,803,800	2,976,400
INCOME BEFORE FIXED CHARGES	1,945,000	3,969,000	4,728,000	5,020,300
Less				
Fixed Charges:				
Ad Valorem Taxes	161,800	277,300	277,300	277,300
Insurance/Building/Cont.	29,000	51,600	54,300	57,100
Reserves	64,100	186,300	282,600	375,000
Total Fixed Charges	254,900	515,200	614,200	709,400
INCOME BEFORE MANAGEMENT				
FEES	1,690,100	3,453,800	4,113,800	4,310,900
Less				
Management Fees:	192,300	372,600	423,900	450,000
INCOME BEFORE DEBT SERVICE	$1,497,800	$ 3,081,200	$ 3,689,900	$ 3,860,900

	1991 70%	1992 70%	1993 70%	1994 70%	1995 70%	1996 70%
	$ 8,253,000	$ 8,762,000	$ 9,302,500	$ 9,876,200	$10,485,400	$11,132,100
	7,095,200	7,532,500	7,997,200	8,490,700	9,014,300	9,570,200
	412,700	438,100	465,100	493,800	524,300	556,600
	165,100	175,200	186,000	197,500	209,700	222,600
	15,926,000	16,907,800	17,950,800	19,058,200	20,233,700	21,481,500
	1,791,800	1,902,400	2,019,600	2,144,000	2,276,400	2,416,800
	5,293,500	5,620,100	5,966,900	6,334,700	6,725,200	7,140,100
	350,800	372,400	395,400	419,700	445,600	473,100
	7,436,100	7,894,900	8,381,900	8,898,400	9,447,200	10,030,000
	8,489,900	9,012,900	9,568,900	10,159,800	786,500	11,451,500
	1,119,300	1,188,500	1,261,500	1,339,300	1,422,100	1,509,500
	643,300	683,000	725,300	769,900	817,500	868,000
	708,200	752,100	798,500	847,700	900,000	955,500
	689,100	731,600	776,800	824,700	875,500	929,500
	3,159,900	3,355,200	3,562,100	3,781,600	4,015,100	4,262,500
	5,330,000	5,657,700	6,006,800	6,378,200	6,771,400	7,189,000
	277,300	277,300	277,300	277,300	277,300	277,300
	60,000	63,100	66,300	69,700	73,200	77,000
	477,800	507,200	538,500	571,700	607,000	644,400
	815,100	847,600	882,100	918,700	957,500	998,700
	4,514,900	4,810,100	5,124,700	5,459,500	5,813,900	6,190,300
	277,800	507,200	538,500	571,700	607,000	644,400
	$4,237,100	$4,302,900	$4,586,200	$4,887,800	$5,206,900	$5,545,900

COMMERCIAL RETAIL BUILDING — 13,300 SQUARE FEET
REPRESENTATIVE PROJECT BUDGET

		Cost Per Sq. Foot	Total Project Cost
Leasable Area (s.f.)	13,300.00		
Land Costs			
Land	$ 57,721.36	$16.00	$ 923,541.70
Net Land	57,721.36		923,541.70
Net Land Cost to Building		69.44	
Development Costs			
Construction Period Taxes		0.68	9,024.05
Contingency		0.80	10,693.20
Developers Fee	(5% of Hard Costs)	2.38	31,649.88
Financing Fees	(1 point)	1.36	18,048.10
Insurance Title Fees		0.63	8,379.00
Lease Commissions		5.40	71,820.00
Legal		0.46	6,118.00
Total Development Costs		11.71	155,732.23
Soft Costs			
Architect and Engineering		2.22	29,478.12
Testing and Inspection		0.70	9,285.40
Total Soft Costs		2.92	38,763.52
Hard Costs			
Shell		38.59	513,311.90
Tenant Finish		11.53	153,299.79
Total Hard Costs		50.12	666,611.69
Total Cost Before Interest			1,784,649.14
Construction Period Interest		12.35	164,255.00
Total Project Costs			$1,948,904.14
Cost Per Square Foot			$146.53

COMMERCIAL RETAIL BUILDING REPRESENTATIVE

	Sq. Ft.	Avg. Rent*	Year 1
Revenues:			
Copy	1,404	$26.97	$ 34,975.00
Furs	780	24.98	18,720.00
Jewelry	1,924	29.32	47,985.00
Restaurant/Bar	5,200	25.00	130,000.00
Retail	1,496	23.87	29,373.00
Retail/Other	1,716	27.38	42,900.00
Travel	780	28.73	19,890.00
Rental Income	13,300	26.21	323,843.00
Less			
Vacancy on retail		.05	9,692.15
Gross Revenue			314,150.85
Operating Expenses			
Management Fee		.04	12,566.03˙
Repair and Maintenance		.05	665.00
Total Operating Expenses			13,231.03
Cash Flow Before			
Debt Service			$300,919.82
Return on Total Cost $1,949,000			15%

*All Leases are Triple Net

13,300 SQUARE FEET PROJECT PRO FORMA

Market Income Year 2	Year 3	Year 4	Year 5
$ 36,352.00	$ 37,913.00	$ 42,204.00	$ 44,933.00
18,720.00	19,656.00	20,835.00	22,086.00
57,582.00	57,720.00	62,337.00	67,325.00
130,000.00	130,000.00	130,000.00	166,400.00
32,033.00	39,155.00	42,288.00	45,671.00
45,474.00	48,048.00	51,480.00	54,568.80
21,388.00	23,232.00	25,116.00	27,125.00
341,549.00	355,724.00	374,260.00	428,108.80
10,577.45	11,286.20	12,213.00	13,085.44
330,971.55	344,437.80	362,047.00	415,023.36
13,238.86	14,228.96	14,970.40	17,124.35
665.00	665.00	665.00	665.00
13,903.86	14,893.96	15,635.40	17,789.35
$317,067.69	$329,543.84	$346,411.60	$397,234.01
16%	17%	18%	20%

INDUSTRIAL BUILDING — 120,000 SQUARE FEET
REPRESENTATIVE PROJECT BUDGET

Land	274,428 S.F. @ $3.00/S.F.		$ 823,284
Shell	120,000 S.F. @ $12.43/S.F.		1,491,600
Finish	120,000 S.F. @ $6.00/S.F.		720,000
Total Hard Costs			$3,034,884
Development Fee			$ 91,047
Interest			
Land		$180,093	
Shell		69,919	
Vacancy		289,361	
Lease Up Income		(75,000)	
Total Interest			$ 464,373
Architecture		$20,000	
Legal		10,000	
Marketing		10,000	
Commission		35,000	
Property Taxes		20,000	
Landscape		35,000	
Contingency		20,000	
Other Cost			$ 150,000
TOTAL COST			$3,740,304
Total Cost/S.F.			$31.17

PRO FORMA

Net Rent	$4.95 S.F.		$ 594,000
Expenses			
Taxes	0.35 S.F.		$ 42,000
Insurance	0.04 S.F.		4,800
Maintenance	0.02 S.F.		2,400
Vacancy	5%		29,700
Management	4%		23,760
Total Expenses			$ 102,660
Pre-Debt Income			$ 491,340
Yield			$ 13.14%
Mortgage Loan			$3,418,017
Equity Requirement			$ 322,286

INDUSTRIAL BUILDING — APPROXIMATELY 118,000 SQUARE FEET
REPRESENTATIVE PROJECT PRO FORMA

Assumptions					
Square Feet	117,415	Property Tax	0.35SF	Land Value	$ 880,260
Ave. Rent PSF	$4.95	Insurance	0.010SF	Building Cost	$2,851,903
Management	3%	Maintenance	0.01SF		
Vacancy	5%	Commissions	0		
Interest Rate	11%	Inflation-Revenue	5%		
		Inflation-Expenses	2%		

	5 Month Stub Period	Year 1	Year 2	Year 3	Year 4
Rental Income	$ 70,715	$ 549,137	$ 585,192	$ 600,090	$ 636,048
Less Vacancy	3,536	27,457	29,260	30,005	31,802
Net Rental Income	67,179	521,680	555,932	570,085	604,246
Expenses:					
Management	2,015	15,650	16,678	17,103	18,127
Maintenance	489	1,198	1,222	1,246	1,271
Property Taxes	17,123	41,917	42,755	43,611	44,483
Insurance	489	1,198	1,222	1,246	1,271
Commissions	805	1,932	1,932	644	0
Total Expenses	20,921	61,895	63,809	63,850	65,152
Pre-Debt Cash Flow	46,258	459,785	492,123	506,235	539,094
Debt Service	165,765	432,250	432,250	432,250	432,250
After Debt Cash Flow	$(119,507)	$ 27,535	$ 59,873	$ 73,985	$ 106,844
Depreciation	61,932	164,950	167,195	166,363	160,988
Taxable Income (Loss)	$(181,439)	$(137,415)	$(107,322)	$ (92,378)	$ (54,144)

Debt — 3,800,000 @ 11.375 Interest Only; 10 Year Term

Year 5	Year 6	Year 7	Year 8	Year 9	Year 10
$ 666,378	$ 712,688	$ 749,782	$ 759,558	$ 779,226	$ 798,320
33,319	35,634	37,489	37,978	38,961	39,916
633,059	677,054	712,293	721,580	740,265	758,404
18,992	20,312	21,369	21,647	22,208	22,752
1,296	1,322	1,349	1,376	1,403	1,431
45,372	46,280	47,206	48,150	49,113	50,095
1,296	1,322	1,349	1,376	1,403	1,431
0	0	0	0	0	0
66,956	69,236	71,273	72,548	74,127	75,709
566,103	607,818	641,020	649,032	666,138	682,695
432,250	432,250	432,250	432,250	432,250	432,250
$ 133,853	$ 175,568	$ 208,770	$ 216,782	$ 233,888	$ 250,445
159,000	157,452	157,452	157,452	152,613	150,505
$(25,147)	$ 18,116	$ 51,318	$ 59,330	$ 81,275	$ 99,940

		Year 11 Sale
Capitalize @ 9.5%		$ 7,481,388
Debt		(3,800,000)
		3,681,388
Sale Proceeds		3,681,388
Capital Gain Tax		(736,278)
Cash		$ 2,945,110

MULTIFAMILY HOUSING — 352 UNITS
REPRESENTATIVE PROJECT BUDGET

A. DEVELOPER'S COST	*Budget*
Land Acquisition Cost	$1,540,000
Design Services	
Architectural Design	70,000
Civil Engineering	7,000
Electrical Engineering	5,000
Landscape Design	4,500
Mechanical Engineering	5,000
Soils Report Fee	1,500
	93,000
Agency and Utility Fees	
Building Permit Fee	330,000
Planning Department Fee	10,000
	340,000
Taxes/Bonds/Insurance/Legal	
Builder's Risk and Fire Insurance	20,000
Real Estate Tax Construction	5,000
	25,000
Financing	
Construction Land Broker Fee	81,375
Construction Land Mortgage Interest	1,313,625
Construction Land Title and Closing	30,000
Equity Brokers Fee	29,000
Permanent Land Broker Fee	83,000
Permanent Land Legal	20,000
Syndication Costs	40,000
	1,597,000
General Overhead	
Advertising and Promotion	30,000
Contractor Fee	210,000
Developer Contingency	176,000
	416,000
DEVELOPER S COST SUB-TOTAL	4,011,000

B. JOBSITE EXPENSE	
Assistant Superintendent	23,000
Auto and Trucks under 4 tons	5,000
Electricity	4,000
Final Cleanup	9,500

	Budget
Gasoline and Oil	9,800
Jobsite Expenses	5,000
Laborer	38,500
Office and Sheds	3,000
Office Engineer	6,200
Office Supplies	600
Photo	350
Repairs	1,200
Sales Taxes	238,000
Scheduling	1,700
Security	12,000
Signs and Bulletin Boards	5,000
Small Equipment etc.	7,200
Small Tools	1,600
Stairways and Platforms	750
Superintendent	77,000
Telephone	4,700
Temporary Fencing	7,800
Toilets	4,100
Trash Cleanup and Disposa	19,800
Vehicle Allowance	10,000
Water	4,000
JOBSITE SUB-TOTAL	499,800

C. SITE WORK	
Accessory Buildings	6,100
Grading	75,100
Landscaping Work	203,000
On-site Roads and Walks	230,200
Patios	10,000
Playground Equipment	0
Fence and Gates	0
Site Improvements/Property Line	20,000
Site Preparation	20,000
Site Utilities	80,900
Swimming Pool and Equipment	92,000
Tennis and Ball Courts	55,000
Trash Areas	10,000
SITE WORK SUB-TOTAL	802,300

D. CONCRETE	Budget
Slabs on Grade	355,000
Concrete Testing	4,000
Lightweight Concrete	69,500
CONCRETE SUB-TOTAL	428,500

E. METALS	
Stairs and Rails / Concrete Treads	71,000
METALS SUB-TOTAL	71,000

F. Carpentry

Finished Carpentry	75,500
Lumber-Dimensional	720,000
Rough Carpentry (Labor) Walls	
Systems	315,000
Wood Trusses	130,000
CARPENTRY SUB-TOTAL	1,240,500

G. ROOFING	
Roofing and Inspection	277,500

H. DOORS AND WINDOWS	
Doors and Frames	155,800
Windows and Glass	79,500
DOORS AND WINDOWS SUB-TOTAL	235,300

I. FINISHES

Floors	210,300
Walls and Ceilings	
Gypsum Wallboard/	
Walls and Ceilings	460,000
Lath, Plaster, and Stucco	500,000
Painting	148,000
Wallpaper	22,600
FINISHES SUB-TOTAL	1,340,900

J. BUILDING SPECIALTIES	Budget
Hardware Items	
Apartment Nos./Letters/	
Signs	1,000
Bath and Toilet	10,000
Fire Extinguishers	6,000
Mailboxes	9,500
Medicine Cabinets	10,000
Mirrors	10,000
BUILDING SPECIALTIES SUB TOTAL	46,500

K. EQUIPMENT	
Appliances	76,000
Dishwasher	15,000
Disposal	82,000
Range	9,200
Range Hood	112,000
Refrigerator	192,000
EQUIPMENT SUB-TOTAL	486,200

L. FURNISHINGS	
Drapes	
Drapes Installed	41,000
Other Personal Property	
Office and Poolside	
Furniture	
FURNISHINGS SUB-TOTAL	30,000
	71,000

M. MECHANICAL	
Plumbing System	530,000
Heating and A/C Systems	385,000
Ventilation System	4,800
MECHANICAL SUB-TOTAL	919,800

N. ELECTRICAL	
Electrical Work	419,500

PROJECT TOTAL	$10,849,800

MULTIFAMILY HOUSING
REPRESENTATIVE PROJECT PRO FORMA

	1984	1985 Year 1	1986 Year 2	1987 Year 3
Income:				
Gross Annual Rents	$ 741,840	$2,336,796	$2,734,051	$3,198,840
($/s.f./mo.)	0.567	0.595	0.697	0.815
(Percentage occupied)	0.90	0.90	0.95	0.95
Rental Income	667,656	2,103,116	2,597,349	3,038,898
Miscellaneous Income	11,984	35,952	35,952	35,952
Total Income	679,640	2,139,068	2,633,301	3,074,850
Operating Expenses				
Operating Expenses	235,658	742,323	779,439	818,411
Management Fees	33,982	107,043	112,395	118,015
Total Operating Expenses	269,640	849,366	891,834	936,426
($/s.f./year)	0.82	2.60	2.73	2.86
Net Operating Income	410,000	1,289,702	1,741,466	2,138,424
Less: Principal 1st Mortgage	0	0	0	0
Principal Line of Credit	0	0	0	7,094
Interest 1st Mortgage	720,400	2,161,200	2,161,200	2,161,200
Interest Line of Credit	0	18,756	147,198	183,880
TOTAL CASHFLOW FROM OPERATIONS	$ (310,400)	$ (890,254)	$ (566,932)	$ (213,750)

1988 Year 4	1989 Year 5	1990 Year 6	1991 Year 7	1992 Year 8	1993 Year 9
$3,390,770	$3,594,217	$3,809,870	$4,038,462	$4,280,770	$4,537,616
0.864	0.916	0.971	1.029	1.091	1.156
0.95	0.95	0.95	0.95	0.95	0.95
3,221,232	3,414,506	3,619,376	3,836,539	4,066,731	4,310,735
35,952	35,952	35,952	35,952	35,952	35,952
3,257,184	3,450,458	3,655,328	3,872,491	4,102,683	4,346,687
859,331	902,298	947,413	994,783	1,044,523	1,096,749
123,916	130,112	136,617	143,448	150,621	158,152
983,247	1,032,410	1,084,030	1,138,232	1,195,143	1,254,900
3.01	3.16	3.31	3.48	3.65	3.84
2,273,937	2,418,048	2,571,298	2,734,259	2,907,540	3,091,787
0	0	0	0	0	0
95,958	85,334	248,824	441,644	653,482	0
2,161,200	2,161,200	2,161,200	2,161,200	2,161,200	2,161,200
183,029	171,514	161,274	131,415	78,418	0
$ (166,250)	$ 0	$ 0	$ 0	$ 14,440	$ 930,587

PROJECT ORGANIZATION

This aspect of every project is the most underestimated in what it can contribute to the project's success. Project Organization is part of the "sense" that a project must have to be undertaken and completed successfully.

Front-end planning on project organization is a must. Written procedures and formalized means of communication can help every project flow smoothly and avoid the "who shot John" problems. This should include:

- Weekly construction status report and job site minutes
- Change order procedures
- Punch list procedures
- Loan draw and payment procedures
- General construction/FF&E breakdown
- Turnover/acceptance
- Tenant improvement procedures
- Property management and security

After organizing the Project Team's communication and work coordination, you need to make certain that you as project owner and developer are properly staffed and structured. We have yet to see anyone overkill being organized and efficient on a major project. Yet, project organization without the business philosophy behind it is like the huge sailing vessel without the rudder. This business philosophy is characterized by:

- Attitudes
- Professionalism and Experience
- Business practices

Attitudes

Some developers will never acknowledge that there is a "pulse" at the job site. This "pulse" can be upbeat, full of "can-do" attitudes and cooperation with everything on top of the table. Or, the "pulse" can be downbeat, with contractors (and even consultants) making mountains out of molehills because the team is not pulling together. Once a project has degenerated to the point where "cover your *$#!x letters" are prevalent, it is difficult to turn it around. Everyone becomes preoccupied with their change orders versus their marching orders.

We are still amazed at the number of consultants and construction team members who refer back to the *espirit de corps* exemplified in 1977-78 when we built the Hyatt Regency Dallas and

Reunion Tower, the first major project that had been undertaken in Downtown Dallas in over 10 years. The average age of our company employees was then 28 years (This figure was averaged up by our 62 year old on-site construction manager!) Our business approach was simple — organize, communicate, treat all people the same, and have fun. There were many who claimed that we were doing business like it used to be done from the old school where craftsmanship was art and everyone could count on each other to perform. So much for the good ol' days, huh?

Make sure that you intertwine key deadlines with some excitement and fun. When the 50 story Reunion Tower was topped out, we gave all the Project Team members an opportunity to have a firm picture taken on the top of the tower with the skyline of Dallas as a background. What better way to reinforce the team's pride in the project? Whether it's baseball caps with the project logo or barbeque at the site after a key event, generate excitement in the project! It pays off many times in quality control and smooth sailing.

Some developers get blamed for not treating all team members the same, and we've seen several projects (again, our competitors) where it looked like the owner had teamed up with the architect against the contractor. One profits by listening to all sides and walking the fine line throughout the project. Otherwise, you *will* get caught in the "who shot John" squabbles.

Whether at the construction site or the consultant's office, know all the Project Team members on a first name basis. This personal touch supports the "one big happy family" concept that keeps job tensions to a minimum. We can remember a story that illustrates this attitude well. At one of our big hotel projects, it was several weeks before opening and it was apparent that the ballroom chandeliers were not going to be installed without extensive overtime. All the electricians were spread everywhere wrapping up the project — hooking up kitchen equipment, punch list work, etc. I was visiting with the electrical foreman about the ballroom status, and I could just feel the set up occurring relative to a change order coming for overtime — from the owner's wallet. Since it was late in the day, I changed subjects by asking the foreman how his sons were doing, and he mentioned that they were getting ready for little league baseball season, but he (as Coach) had not yet found a $500 sponsor for their little league team. Feeling that I had nothing to lose, I casually mentioned that if the ballroom chandeliers were finished on time, I would personally fork over the bucks to sponsor the team. You should have seen the next day at the job — the ballroom was a beehive of electricians. It was like a volcanic eruption. Not only was the ballroom finished early, but somehow I missed out being asked to pay for a change order for several thousand dollars of unnecessary overtime. Not only was this the best $500 contribution I ever made, but the baseball team went on to the state playoffs!

Experience and Professionals

Our firm has always been composed primarily of business school people with minimal in-house staff. Consequently, our business approach has always been to find and hire the best consultants and contractors. Furthermore, our firm's business practices and way of doing business have put us at the top of consultants' and contractors' lists of people they want to do business with. We contend strongly that "the system works," and our jobs are done with better workmanship at more competitive prices. Yet, it first comes down to the people you do business with — the Project Team — and we've previously mentioned some of the selection criteria.

Rather than give you some generalities, we want to discuss twenty common mistakes that typically recur over and over. These point up the need for going with experience. These items don't include financing issues since without financing, you don't have a project anyway.

Twenty Common Mistakes (to either avoid or increase the budget to accommodate)

1. *Incomplete design* — The Project Team must agree on when they have enough information to adquately price the project; otherwise, watch out for change orders ("got cha").
2. *Approvals* — Many times the owner fails to approve the design features on a timely basis. It is up to the architect and contractor to make sure these are obtained when needed. Otherwise, delays mount up as work schedules get thrown out of sequence.
3. *Mock ups and samples* — Mock ups and samples are needed to portray the finished appearance and the design effect that is being desired. Otherwise, the project is brought to a standstill waiting for the owner to pick something else while the workmen are tearing down off the building what the owner does not like.
4. *Utilities* — Lack of adequate utilities to serve the job site (sewer, water, drainage, temporary and permanent electrical power, phone service to handle the line capacity and data transmission requirements).
5. *Elevators* — inadequate elevator service is provided during the construction period, thereby creating a situation where time is wasted while workers are waiting for vertical transportation bet-

ween floors. Also, the ball is dropped many times as to who picks up the elevator maintenance service after the permanent elevators have been accepted but prior to the turning over of the project to the operations people.

6. *Storage* — Inadequate storage facilities for construction materials at the job site compared to how the project is to be phased. This would include both outside storage (construction trailers, building materials, etc.) as well as inside secured storage (equipment, parts, etc.).

7. *Electrical conduit* — Lack of sufficient conduit for electrical needs as well as all other forms of communications and property management equipment.

8. *Delivery and control points* — No set procedures are identified for the receipt and distribution of construction materials and daily goods and services provided to the job site. Typically, an equipment truck shows up at the site and the driver talks with at least 20 people before the right person is identified to know where the truck needs to unload. (This usually works out to be the construction superintendent, who is the last person that you want to get involved in this matter).

9. *Structural check* — The contractor did not make an independent structural check on the plans and specifications to make sure that it met his own building standards (any prudent contractor would have done this anyway, right?)

10. *Security* — Lack of sufficient security at the job site which should be increased regularly during the construction period. Sometimes, contractors think security is a 4 foot high cyclone fence and a retired person sleeping in a car during the night outside the job site offices.

11. *Clean up* — Lack of the job being free of construction debris. Trash should be picked up on a daily basis. This is usually brought to your attention when several construction workers can't find their tools the next morning because trash is everywhere.

12. *Rain leaks* — The building is not sufficiently closed in to stop leaks nor have recurring leaks been properly corrected. If the building contractor does the finish work, the amount of leaks in the building will be inversely proportionate to the amount of tenant finish work he has done!

13. *Lender requirements* — Lack of understanding on the front end by the contractor of how the lending agreements work as well as the legal requirements that occur such as assignment of the construction contract, subordination, etc.

14. *Punch list* — Lack of organized punch list procedures or punch lists occuring on a current basis. (Jobs rarely get a completed punch list after they're opened.) A "punch list" is a list of items yet to be completed on a project that is ready for occupancy. They are the contractor's "loose ends" to be completed before Final Acceptance by the owner.

15. *Central plant* — Lack of attention to not only the start up, but fine tuning of the overall central plant operations prior to opening. Also, lack of coordination between the operations and property management people responsible for maintaining the central plant.

16. *Budget cuts* — Knowing which items to cut from the budget and when to cut them during the budget review process. Many items are subsequently added back later ("I told you so.") — but at a higher price.

17. *Retainage* — Lack of major work and punch list being complete before retainaged is released. Both the contractor and his subcontractors work for the owner. You control the retainage. The retainage is money held in reserve out of the construction contract to assure *all* work is completed satisfactorily. It is released near the time of occupancy and final acceptance.

18. *Future requirements* — Lack of attention both to the future changes that can occur on the project and to the provision of systems, conduit or utilities to serve the future requirements. Everything is less expensive on the front end, versus after the fact.

19. *Poor communication* — Lack of weekly job site meetings, minutes and action items lists to determine "who" is supposed to do "what."

20. *Quality* — Lack of specifications in sufficient detail to leave a very clear understanding of what was supposed to be included in the bid price. It is always interesting to see how semantics work relative to the word "quality" when the specifications are completed after the general construction contract has been signed.

BUSINESS PRACTICES

Don't assume anything or take anything for granted

Our firm had to utilize this principle as a necessity because of our age "problem." We can remember on one of our projects where we bid out the landscaping work to be done at the completion of the project. This project was bid out to our general contractor, a large union shop firm who was capable of doing big things in big ways. This bid was requested out of a sense of courtesy because our construction people had already ruled out the general contractor being interested. The project was also bid to a small local nonunion landscape company with a cigar chewing owner who would flip you for a dime. Any guesses on who came in with the low bid on the project? The general contractor. He had the most to gain and the most to lose, but none of our people were thinking about it from that standpoint.

Don't cry wolf

On many jobs, people play games with dates and deadlines and information that is needed. Don't ever get caught up in that. Credibility is one of the most difficult things to change once it has gone downhill. I can still remember, on the Hyatt Regency Dallas project, when we had our first critical owner/tenant finish date. It was the commencement of the carpet installation. We had pushed the contractor for several months and had given him the exact date that we were going to begin the carpet installation. At 10:00 a.m. on the date that we had requested, a big semi-trailer truck full of carpet from Atlanta was parked outside the general contractor's construction offices ready to be unloaded. We had no credibility problems about delivering on our end throughout the rest of the project.

Provide active owner representation

It sometimes appears on many projects that the owner/developer's active involvement decreases dramatically after the loan has closed and the first funding has occurred on the project. As the developer fades away, the budget jumps up.

Payments

Pay on the same day every month, and make sure that the contractor is also paying his subcontractors on a set basis. Too many things are happening on the job for everyone to worry about when they are going to get paid. (The old "check is in the mail" routine stinks!)

Chief Financial Officer

Either have one, or hire one. Any major project has got to have financial controls and standards commensurate with the activity levels and transaction levels that are anticipated.

Inspections

Make inspections off site to make sure that the marble or granite is being cut on a timely basis or the mullions for the building are being extruded as scheduled. I can still recall the positive impact when our key people went to the PPG corporate offices and manufacturing plant during some difficult times to make sure that we would be receiving our building glass shipments on time and to our quality standards.

Operating people

Get them involved and make sure that you take the building over sooner than later.

SUMMARY

Developing the *right* budget requires attention to detail and hard work. Meeting the budget not only requires the same attention to detail but involves the creation and maintenance of *espirit de corps.* Finally, not only enthusiasm, but a strong hands-on management philosophy must pervade the project by the Owner, his staff, and all members of the Project Team.

C. E. "Doc" Cornutt is executive vice-president and chief financial officer of Hunt Oil Company, one of the largest independent oil companies in the United States. He is also vice president of its affiliated company, Hunt Investment Corporation. Hunt Investments, through its subsidiary Woodbine Development Corporation, has developed almost 3000 acres of industrial, commercial and mixed use parks in the Dallas-Fort Worth area. Hunt also has developed and owns 3,000,000 square feet of office buildings and hotel properties, and 250,000 square feet of warehouse properties.

Lawrence A. Wilson

THE MOST FOR THE CONSTRUCTION DOLLAR

The enhancements of a proposed development resulting from the acquisition of excellent property and the preparation of a quality design can easily be eroded, even lost, through the failure to effectively administer the construction phase of the development. Construction creates the physical being of a development. Poorly planned for and administered, it also creates tremendous problems.

This chapter deals with the procurement of construction and the administration of the construction phase of a project. It describes the various methods of construction procurement and delivery, types of construction contracts, and the best approach to controlling the construction of a project. It does not make the reader an expert on construction but provides a basic understanding of the construction process from purchase through project completion.

The term, "development team," will be used often in this chapter to discuss the development group of owner and/or developer, architect, engineers, consultants and contractor or construction manager. Development team also properly infers a team-like atmosphere and attitude of all working together in harmony toward a common objective of the best possible development. It is important that the developer address the selection of all the respective team members to achieve this team-like attitude and compatability. This should be the goal whether the construction services are to be provided through negotiations or lump sum bidding.

Today, many large developers like Gerald Hines, Cadillac Fairview, and The Rouse Company have the organizational capability to effectively control the design and construction processes. It is important to recognize that the capability to control these processes demands far more expertise than managing the general contractor. It is essential that the developer have a qualified staff, a thorough knowledge of the design/construct process, a strong capability in procedure planning and perhaps most importantly, be represented by a person who has the authority to make decisions and is timely in making those decisions. This tells us a great deal about the organizational needs of the developer; yet, it is amazing how few developers truly have these capabilities within their organization.

The person or persons charged with the responsibility to administer the design and construction processes does not have to be an entrepreneur and, as a matter of fact, that person does not even have to be a trained architect or engineer. The entrepreneur developer may not have the interest and aptitude and probably does not have the time to sit through long design development and construction meetings. The person does need to have a detailed knowledge of the process of designing and constructing projects. The person must be quantitatively analytical and know how to ask questions and what questions to ask. Asking questions of the designers and contractor often leads to new insights and innovations that sometimes produces important competitive advantages for a development. A smartly designed development depends critically on knowing the reasons why certain things are being proposed. Probing — asking questions — is the intuitive search for the logic of, for example: building massing, facade design, or a core layout that data analysis might miss or bury. The ability to question details or designs that are being proposed and *why* is a qualitative capability along with the quantitative analysis capability so important to the effective management of the development process.

Outstanding designers and construction companies do not by themselves make for the successful construction of a development. Essential to the development team is the developer representative who has the authority to act, give direction, and make decisions for the developer and also, as mentioned previously, be responsive and timely in making those decisions. It is often and correctly said that more time can be lost in the design phase of a project than in the construction phase. While the designers are more likely to be blamed for this lost time, it is most often the indecisiveness or the lack of authority of the developer's representative that causes the loss in time.

It becomes clear that one of the keys to a developer's ability to control the design and construction processes is the person or persons in the organization that are responsible for those activities. If the developer or his representative are lacking in any of these required skills, then it is important that they be supplemented through the retention of consultants. If the architect or contractor has the needed capability, these skills may be contracted from them.

The delivery of construction services can be achieved through a number of different methods. The decision as to which is the most appropriate method will be influenced by considerations of many issues including:

- Complexity of the development
- Construction knowledge and administration capability of the developer's staff
- Timing demands and constraints for the development
- Capabilities of available construction firms
- Capability and role of the architects and engineers
- The market place for contracting, labor, and materials
- Financial constraints

Regardless of which of the following construction delivery methods are used, the most appropriate and best qualified organization to carry out the work is a general contractor. The exception to this would be where the developer's needs suggest that a construction consultant be employed to supplement his own organization. A properly selected general contractor should have the experienced personnel, estimating capability, management systems, and construction savvy — all of the necessary tools to best perform the required work.

The following delivery methods are the most prevalent in the industry, particularly private commercial construction.

DESIGN-BID-CONSTRUCT APPROACH

This is the traditional approach of the architect/engineer designing the project and preparing the completed plans and specifications. Once complete, competitive bids are secured from four to six general contractors for the construction services, which are based on the plans and specifications.

Contract: While several construction contract options are available, the type most used in this approach to construction delivery is the lump sum fixed price contract with a single source of responsibility, the general contractor. The fixed price contract is an agreement to perform the defined construction work at a set price regardless of the cost to the contractor. It is important to call the reader's attention to the advantage in private work of prequalifying and selecting the list of bidders. A properly selected list of bidders will eliminate many potential problems during the construction phase of the project. Verification of contractor references is essential.

Developer Responsibilities

1. Provide comprehensive and complete construction documents.
2. Provide the organizational expertise or consultants with proficiency in providing direction to the design team in the areas of planning, scheduling, conceptual budgeting, systems analysis, cost control, and bid analysis.
3. Inspection and construction administration personnel to evaluate the in-progress work and the performance of the general contractor and architect/engineer.

Advantages

1. A complete set of construction documents prior to receiving bids or proposals which should minimize the potential for claims and change order requests arising from a poorly defined scope of work.
2. The design-bid-construct approach provides the maximum opportunity for competitive pricing on a project because the contractors, subcontractors, and suppliers are utilizing what should be a comprehensive and complete set of construction documents for the basis of their bids.
3. This approach requires less staffing by the developer, particularly in the areas of accounting and auditing.
4. The established roles of owner, architect/engineer, and general contractor are maintained through this approach and terms of the typical contract agreements and general conditions to the contract have been long established through construction contract law.

Disadvantages

1. The design-bid-construct approach is the most *linear* of all construction delivery systems and consequently, is the most lengthy.
2. This approach is the longest because of being linear, but it is often further extended when the design cost control effort is not effective. If it is discovered at bid time that the project is over budget, the required value engineering, redesign, and repricing further extends the time requirement.
3. The developer does not enjoy the benefit of the general contractor's input on planning, scheduling, budgeting and cost control during the design phases of the project. There is not a full team approach to the project.
4. Because it is best to have complete construction documents at the time bids are taken, the developer has a large investment of time and dollars in the project before the price has been established.

5. Due to the competitive market place and the natural approach of a general contractor to search for every possible advantage over his bid competition, the successful contractor and the developer are often placed in adversary positions in the implementation of the construction work.

TEAM APPROACH

Description: The developer selects a general contractor at the beginning of the conceptual design phase through negotiations and a qualifications oriented selection process. The developer contracts with the contractor to provide expertise in such areas as planning, scheduling, budgeting, systems analysis, and cost control during the design phase and construction services during the construction phase of the project. On many public type projects, the team approach is used with the role of the contractor type being called a construction manager. Obviously, there are many statutory constraints on the role of a construction manager on public type work, particularly the public bid process. A private developer would not be restricted in this way.

The team approach is used to gain the expertise of all the traditional parties (developer, architect/engineer, and contractor) in a continuous development process throughout the design and construction phases of the project. It eliminates the adversary relationship and the related problems that are often prevalent in the design-bid-construct approach. This approach or variation thereof, is the one most commonly used by developers on commercial work today.

Contract: The contractor services in the team approach are usually contracted through a fixed fee, cost reimbursable, or payroll multiple type arrangement during the design phases of the project. When sufficient construction documents are available, a cost reimbursable with guaranteed maximum price type contract is executed for the construction phase. The guaranteed maximum contract is an agreement to perform the work and be reimbursed on the basis of actual cost plus a stipulated fee with the contractor guaranteeing not to exceed the maximum price.

A typical guaranteed maximum contract will include an incentive savings clause to induce the contractor to put forth a best effort to realize savings in the cost of construction. Today, most contracts used for this type of work are derived from the AIA 111, "Cost of the Work Plus a Fee", contract form.

Developer Responsibilities

1. Provide a representative who has the knowledge, responsibility, involvement, and decisiveness to make prompt decisions after

studying the team's recommendations.

2. Select architect/engineers who understand the *team approach,* are willing to function as team members, and who will be receptive to evaluating recommendations and suggested alternatives made by the contractor.
3. Select a general contractor who has the management experience and philosophy to participate as a team member and who has the skill and knowledge to provide planning, develop schedules, perform budgeting, analyze alternative designs, advise concerning construction techniques and perform value engineering.
4. Be an involved team member throughout the process — by participating as much as required to insure the orderly flow of the team's effort.

Advantages

1. The development benefits from the involvement and interaction of all members of the development team from the beginning of the planning and design phases through construction.
2. The development of a team-like atmosphere among the participants, creates a better project.
3. The participation of a general contractor or construction manager during planning and design provides expertise in areas like construction feasibility, cost control, scheduling, alternative designs and value engineering.
4. It is possible to start the project earlier (fast track or phased construction) before all construction documents are complete, and in doing so, provide the opportunity for savings in both time and interest and inflation costs.
5. It provides the developer early-on knowledge of the cost of the proposed design for the development, which enables the developer to determine the financial feasibility of the project long before construction documents are completed. As a result, major portions of the design expense can be saved until financial feasibility has been established.
6. It allows greater flexibility to pre-award or pre-purchase certain parts of work, materials, or equipment which require a long lead time for delivery.
7. It is the best approach for the developer to realize the most economical cost, and to deliver the project in the shortest time period.

Disadvantages

1. There is not the advantage of competitive bidding among a selected list of qualified contractors.
2. Construction documents are typically not complete at the time the guaranteed maximum price is prepared and the construction contract is executed. This places an extra burden on the contractor and architect/engineers to insure the cost of the work does not

grow as a result of design definition and the development of working drawings.

3. When the contract documents are not fully defined, there is the potential for conflicts with the contractor as to what items added in construction document definition are original scope and what are extras.

4. When budget costs are established during the conceptual or schematic phases of design, the issues of costs and costs vs. quality can create conflicts between the contractor and architect/engineer members of the team.

CONSTRUCTION CONSULTANT

This delivery approach involves the utilization of a construction consultant in lieu of a general contractor or construction manager providing construction input for design decisions during the design phases of a project. The construction consultant may leave the development team following the planning and design phases or he may continue as an advisor to or agent of the developer during the construction phase of the development. The services of a general contractor are required during the construction phase.

The construction consultant is typically used by developers who lack strong design and construction administration expertise in their in-house staff.

Contract: A professional services type contract is similar in format to the architect's contract used for contracting with the construction consultant. The financial basis of the contract can be a stipulated sum or multiple of payroll; however, the stipulated sum is normally used.

Developer Responsibilities

1. Provide comprehensive and complete construction documents.
2. Provide inspection and construction administration personnel to evaluate the work-in-progress and the performance of the general contractor and architect/engineer.

Advantages

1. Like the team approach with the general contractor or construction manager, the developer is gaining construction related expertise during the design phases of the project.

Disadvantages

1. The construction consultant does not perform the actual construction of the project so he is not in a position of having to stand by the costs, material and equipment recommendations, and schedules that he has prepared, as opposed to the general

contractor who guarantees them through the execution of a guaranteed maximum or lump sum construction contract.

2. The construction consultant adds another entity to the team and is often in an adversary relationship with the general contractor and the architect/engineers.

DESIGN/BUILD APPROACH

The developer contracts with a single entity to provide both design services and construction services. The contracting entity may, in turn, subcontract part of the work if the design/build entity does not have all of the capabilities within the existing organization. For instance, a general contractor may contract to design/build a project, then subcontract the design work to an architect/engineering firm.

In all the previously discussed construction delivery approaches, the levels of performance are established through the development of a design concept, then pricing for the project tracks the design development. In the design/build approach, often the price is established first, based upon a performance criteria and the design work follows.

The design/build approach is more prevalent in the delivery of manufacturing and industrial facilities, although it is used by some retail developers today on shopping centers. It is also often utilized in some areas of the country for the mechanical and electrical components of commercial projects.

Contract: The best agreement for design-build services is a guaranteed maximum or upset price contract with the design-build contractor being reimbursed on the basis of actual cost plus a fee and guarantee that the maximum price will not be exceeded.

Developer Responsibility

1. Strong capabilities to evaluate proposals and prepare cost/benefit analysis.
2. Provide a well prepared, extremely thorough program and performance criteria to establish the guidelines for design, quality and function for all areas of the proposed project.
3. Understanding that the commitment is made to the cost of the project prior to having a detailed design to support those costs.
4. Inspection and construction administrative personnel to evaluate the work-in-progress and the performance of the design/build contractor.

Advantages:

1. Single point contract responsibility for design and construction.
2. Minimize potential communication problems by integrating the design and construction tasks.

3. The early on establishment of a firm price for the design and construction of the project.
4. The ability to start the project earlier if desired before all construction documents are complete and in doing so, provide the opportunity for both time and cost savings.
5. The ability to pre-award or pre-purchase certain areas of the work and materials requiring long lead time.
6. Economical and time efficient approach to development.

Disadvantages

1. The developer loses the check and balance system of developer, architect/engineer, and contractor in their more traditional relationships.
2. The developer does not have the same flexibility in obtaining desired design features as in more traditional approaches to construction delivery.
3. There is a potential deficiency in the aesthetic design quality using the design/build approach.

These are four basic approaches to the delivery of construction services. There are many variations to each and you will find all types of variations and combinations being utilized by developers in the market-place today. The selection of the appropriate approach depends upon the developer's organization capabilities and the requirements of the proposed development. Without question, the team approach in one form or other is the most favored approach today by developers of commercial type projects. It is the favorite because of the many advantages it offers to the development team including the determination of financial feasibility prior to major outlay of time and design expenses, the ability to control the costs of the project, and the least linear or shortest in time.

Unfortunately, too often we see developers trying to take advantage of the team approach but using competitive bids to select the general contractor member of the team. The team approach and the design — bid — construct approach are both excellent methods of construction delivery, but they don't mix very well. The reason is that for a developer to take bids from even a carefully selected list of bidders on schematic documents or partially completed working drawings, the developer is placing himself in an extremely vulnerable position that will almost inevitably lead to problems, disputes and possibly claims. Incomplete documents invite omissions, misinterpretations, errors in judgement — all the things that generate disputes.

We don't know of any developer organization, even those with outstanding construction administration staffs, that have the

ability to sufficiently analyze bids based upon significantly incomplete documents and insure proper contract protection. It
simply cannot be done. When using the team approach, the contractor or construction manager should be selected on the overall
evaluation of his qualifications to perform the work required, including the ability to be cost competitive. A lump sum price is not
an effective method of evaluating the contractor's qualifications.

There are certain criteria a developer should look for in selecting a general contractor or construction manager. Regardless of
whether you are selecting qualified bidders for lump sum bidding
on your project or selecting the contractor member of the team
where the team approach is to be employed, the developer is looking for the same basic qualifications with only slight variations.
The principal qualifications are:

CONTRACTOR QUALIFICATIONS FOR LUMP SUM BID

1. Successful completion of similar projects (type, size, complexity,
   etc.)
2. Experience and capability of the contractor's personnel who are
   available for assignment in the key positions, including project
   manager, project engineers, project superintendent and others as
   required.
3. Capability of the contractor to take on the proposed project given
   his existing and contemplated work load.
4. Quality of management systems including construction planning,
   scheduling, field administration and field procedures and safety
   programs.
5. Financial capability and responsibility. Can the contractor provide a performance and payment bond if required? Does he have
   the available working capital to asure the financial stability for
   his work?
6. Reputation in the industry, including the ability to work
   cooperatively with owners, developers, architects, engineers and
   subcontractors.
7. Does he have the reputation of being a "claims" contractor?
8. Strength of insurance programs and insurance ratings.
9. Knowledge of the market place and labor conditions where the
   project is to be constructed.

CONTRACTOR QUALIFICATIONS FOR
THE TEAM APPROACH

Without exception, all of the above contractor qualifications
are important in evaluating the contractor's ability to perform in
the team apprach. However, there are a number of additional
qualifications necessary for the team approach. Additional exper-

tise is required of a contractor working on the team beyond that required of a lump sum bid contractor. There are many excellent lump sum bid contractors who do not have the expertise to operate in the team approach, and are not effective in that role. These additional experience requirements are:

1. The ability to function effectively in a team-like environment with the developer, architect, engineers and other consultants.
2. In-depth knowledge of the planning and design processes.
3. Capabilty of the contractor's organization to perform effective budgeting, conceptual estimating and systems evaluations when there are little or no drawings to support the effort.
4. Ability to provide meaningful input for cost control, value engineering, building techniques and purchasing.
5. Reputation for on time and within budget delivery of the construction of projects.

It is important to again emphasize the need for cooperation and capability of team members. Not all construction firms or architects have the personality or philosophy to work in a team and some architects even resent being placed in this type of organizational structure. However, with the trememdous number of developers using the team approach and also the increased stress on higher design quality for the projects, even the so-called "designer architects" are learning the process.

The selection of the best contractor for a specific project requires careful evaluation of each contractor's capabilities. A fairly simple process can be established to enable the developer to effectively evaluate and screen the prospective contractors:

1. A written invitation is presented to the prospective contractors to determine their interest and request their qualifications. The request for qualifications proposals should include:
   • Name and location of development
   • Architect and engineers, if selected
   • A brief description of the project
   • Estimated start and completion date
   • Approximate construction cost
   • Type of services desired
2. The contractors respond with their expression of interest and qualification proposals covering:
   • Background information on firm
   • Experience
   • Current backlog
   • Proposed project organization and staffing
   • Services to be provided
   • Capability to manage project (Systems)

- Supplemental information that may be of assistance
- References

3. The developer analyzes the contractor submissions, checks on references, past performance, experience, etc.
4. If the contractors are being selected for a lump sum bid project, the prospective list would be reduced to the four to six best qualified contractors.
5. If the contractors are being selected for a team approach, then the prospective list should be reduced to two or possibly three, and those contractors interviewed.

Unfortunately, today you often see too much emphasis being placed upon the presentations at the interview and consequently, the prospective contractors are being evaluated on their ability to put on a side show and not on the basis of their qualifications to provide construction input to the design team and construct the project. The interview is important because it provides the developer the best opportunity to evaluate the prospective contractor's proposed key staff members and the ability to relate and work with them. For this reason, the contractor should be requested to bring the key members of his organization to the interview. Along with the financial capability to perform a project, the contractor's project personnel and those supporting the project staff are the contractor's most important assets.

The developer evaluates and ranks the prospective contractors based upon their qualifications and the specific needs for the project. The contractor with the highest ranking would then meet with the developer to negotiate an appropriate contract fee.

FEE

It would be negligent to write about buying construction services and not talk about construction fees. I have participated in nine or ten seminars on construction management sponsored by the AGC and without exception, at those seminars, whenever the question and answer period came around, the majority of questions related to fees. It's an important topic for everyone including the developer.

The contractor should be selected on his qualifications, not his fee, unless of course, the fee quoted is out of line. A slight difference in fee can be made up ten-fold in superior performance and on schedule delivery.

The fee should properly reflect the caliber of services being proposed. A contractor must also consider the number and qualifications of the necessary staff for the project, the degree of difficulty of the project, project duration and monetary risks in establishing the fee.

When using the team approach, the standard method of setting the fee is on a percentage of the cost of construction. If construction documents are sufficiently developed, then it is reasonable to establish the fee as a stipulated sum.

Construction fees are very much market driven and consequently fluctuate significantly depending on market conditions in a given area. The developer needs to negotiate fees with caution because they can also vary significantly depending on the "reimbursable" in a cost reimbursable contract. It is not unusual for a developer to pay a much higher real fee than what may be set forth in the contract because under the reimbursable the contractor is being paid for costs that, in fact, should be considered fee and were covered by the fee quoted by other contractors.

In this chapter, we have talked about the need for strong and decisive leadership from the developer's organization in both the design and construction phases of a project, the basic methods for delivering construction services, and qualifications to look for when selecting a contractor. In other words, we have our development team put together and we are ready to start the design/construction process.

CONTROL OF THE PROCESS (COSTS)

With the selection of the right architect/engineers and the selection of the best qualified contractor, whether through negotiations or bids from an invited list of bidders, control of the process becomes the key to controlling construction costs. The best method of realizing the most for your construction dollars is through the team approach to construction delivery. A developer who is represented by a qualified person or persons and who has done a good job in selecting qualified team members, has taken a long step toward the control of the process and the resulting control of costs.

It is important that one of the first priorities of the development team should be to establish a target budget price (cost model) for the project. This should be done by the developer or if he lacks that expertise, it should be jointly agreed upon by members of the development team. Everyone needs to know what cost constraints are on the project and have a cost model to work towards. This does not mean the budget won't change — if often does, but not having a cost model to work toward is like starting a sailboat race without a rudder. You can't steer the boat to the finish line.

Another important task is the preparation of a development schedule early in the design phase that would detail design effort as well as the construction work. The schedule then becomes the road map for the team in setting direction as well as tracking the progress of the development. As important as an overall development schedule is to a project, we are constantly surprised at how often major developments are launched without one. The schedule should be a time scaled vector diagram type that shows the interrelationship and dependence between the activities and events of the schedule. Too often schedules are not prepared for the design phase or are prepared and then forgotten. The schedule for the design work is just as important as the schedule for the construction work. The failure to make timely decisions about the design or the selection of key components and materials can easily impact the process of the work as much or more so than events that may take place during the construction of the project. In real estate development, time has severe cost ramifications, whether it is increased fees, inflation in construction costs, or additional interest carry for the cost of money. Time can have a tremendous negative impact on the ultimate cost of a project. For example, the per day increased costs for the delay in completion of a $50 million project will be as much as $20,000 to $25,000 per day, which is reason enough for all team members to be concerned about dedication to schedule.

Control of the conceptual, schematic, and design development phases of the design of a project are key to the ultimate control of the cost of the project. Strong open interaction between all the members of the development team is essential during these phases. Here is when the project should be designed verbally in terms of materials, quality, and performance — and costed before any significant drawing effort takes place. If a proposed design won't fit the cost model at this stage, there is no reason to put it in the working drawings and specifications.

The design is the responsiblity of the architect/engineers. However, the construction consultant, contractor or construction manager has the responsibility of informing the team about cost and time implications of proposed design schemes. The team must be organized and function in a way that construction-related information is inputed to the design effort and proposed designs can be evaluated for their impact on cost and schedules. It is essential to the process that the construction related input be provided as designs are being considered and before design decisions are made — not as a reaction to design decisions after they are made. To accomplish this, the designers and contractor must work together before presenting recommendations and alternatives.

The contractor should analyze proposed systems and subsystems, i.e., foundations, structure, exterior cladding, vertical transportation, heating ventilating and air conditioning, power distribution, etc. — all the systems that make up a building before they are committed to design. This information is provided to the architect/engineers and developer so knowledgeable decisions can be made and dollars spent where they can best benefit development. Again, a caution to the reader that the team must operate in a way that cost and time impact is studied and systems and subsystems are analyzed before design decisions are made; otherwise, there is a strong probability the final design will not be as efficient as it could have been.

A critical point for the developer to keep in mind relating to the cost of a development is the efficiency of a building. Too often, we see owners or developers presented with conceptual or schematic designs by the architect that are truly outstanding from a shape, massing or aesthetic standpoint. The developer falls in love with the design, then finds out too late it's inefficient and cannot compete in the marketplace.

Efficiency comes in numerous ways in a development. For example, the cost per gross square foot of a commercial building means very little. The far more important figure is the cost per useable or rentable square foot. Many buildings have great cost per gross square foot, but are totally inefficient. They have a very poor cost per usable square foot. In hotels and motels, the developer must be concerned about the gross square foot or area per room or "key." If the design varies far from established guidelines, the project will almost certainly have cost problems. Efficiency relates to other areas of a project besides usable square footage. It is affected by form, shape, and layout. The layout of the core of a multi-story building affects almost every operational function of the building in addition to the construction cost of the building. A poorly designed core can result in excessive structural, mechanical, electrical, and even finishing costs. It also impacts the layout of leased spaces, building maintenance, and operating costs. Smart buildings are the ones that are efficient and also have quality aesthetic designs.

Value engineering is the term used to describe a work effort to reduce construction costs that takes place after many of the major design decisions have been made. Like "construction management," it is a term that was first used by the Federal Government. Value engineering is the careful and detailed study of the proposed design of a project, the purpose of which is to develop ways to reduce project cost without a resulting decrease in the real value of the project so that designs can be accomplished in a different way at less cost with a comparable end product. Like conceptual estimating in the early design phases, it requires expertise that not all contractors possess. It is an important task that should be carried out on every project, even if the project costs are within budget.

In order to best insure that project costs are, in fact, being controlled as the design effort is taking place, at least two milestone or budget confirmation estimates should be prepared. The architect/engineer's design work is typically accomplished in cycles — from conceptual to schematic to design development to working drawings. As the design work takes place in these cycles, the level of detail increases and the basis for a contractor's estimating should also improve. Typically, these cost control estimates are developed at the completion of what the architects term the schematic phase and the design development phase. If the budget confirmation estimates indicate problems, then the team must immediately analyze the situation and perform whatever value engineering is necessary to correct the anticipated cost overrun and place the project back within the budget.

When the team is working with the architect/engineers to develop the design for the project, they need to be aware of a number of key external considerations that can have a significant impact on the cost and schedule of the work. The marketplace for buying construction, the availability of certain skilled labor, and the availability of various materials and systems must be investigated before design and selections are finalized. One can quickly understand that it would be a tragic mistake to design a welded steel frame when there was a shortage of qualified welders, or to select a granite facing only to discover that the quarry production is overcommitted. Amazing and as unforgiveable as it may seem to the reader, these mistakes are fairly common. It is also not unusual for a developer or his designer to proceed to select a material (such as a special metal alloy for the curtain wall) cost and delivery problems, but hoping that somehow they will disappear. It is the obligation of all members of the development team to work together to prevent this from happening.

Timing is another consideration in the effective control of project costs. When to purchase an element of the project, when to bid the construction, and when to establish the Guaranteed Maximum Cost. The right timing is obviously dependent on many issues. The degree of completeness of the construction documents, the marketplace, the credibility of the development, the reputations of the developer and architect/engineers, the schedule for construction start, the expected project duration, and even the time of year bids are to be received are some of the many issues that can impact the price of construction. A developer can usually depend on the premise that the most optimum time to purchase construction services for his project is when he has an adequately defined set of documents, and he is confident that the start of the project is a reality. Many times, we have seen the loss of a competitive opportunity in purchasing a project because of numerous false or delayed starts. The contractor, subcontractors, and suppliers become discouraged and lose confidence in the reality of the project.

FAST-TRACK DELIVERY

The more traditional approach of preparing the construction documents for a project and then starting construction is often-times replaced today with the approach of phasing or fast tracking the construction. To fast track a project, the developer starts construction on the respective areas of work as the designs for those areas are substantially completed. This may be long before the design of the total project is completed. An example would be to start excavation, soil retention systems, and foundations. Then as structural drawings are completed, proceed with that work — and so forth, on through the project. In order to accomplish fast-tracking, the architect/engineers develop documents for a sub-system or system. They are priced and construction work starts while the architect/engineers move on to complete the design of other portions of the project.

There are a number of advantages to fast tracking the design and construction of a project in addition to a compressed schedule that obviously saves time. Purchasing and construction starts can be scheduled to best meet market and project conditions. Finish work design may be deferred to eliminate the impact of potential changed design decisions until later in the project. Equipment and materials contracts requiring long lead time can be awarded early. These are the advantages of fast tracking. Unfortunately, unless skillfully managed and controlled, the disadvantatges often outweigh the advantages.

The potential for problems is great when the fast-track approach is used. The best intentions of a super development team can often turn to frustration, defensiveness, and adversary positions among the team members. The developer needs to keep several facts in mind when considering the use of the phased or fast track approach to project delivery. The first fact is that construction is starting before the total cost for the project has been set. The second fact is that by using this approach to project delivery, the design for certain areas of work are being fixed because construction is taking place. However, the designs for the remainder of the work may not be complete, so flexibility of changing a portion of the building is lost — because it is already built! The developer is committing to dollars and designs without knowing the end product in either total cost or final design.

Fast tracking a project places a tremendous burden on the development team to make the correct decisions in the conceptual and schematic design phases of a project, because some degree of flexibility is lost. To remake design decisions will almost certainly result in change orders to the construction contract.

Change orders in the design-bid-construct approach to construction delivery represent an opportunity for the contractor to increase profit margin. With the team approach, change orders are a nuisance and generally create problems, not opportunity.

Change orders generally result from lack of definition, omissions, or conflicts in the contract documents, or the developer or architect/engineer remaking design decisions. Too often, they result from the architect/engineers continuing to fine tune or upgrade their design. Change orders cannot be avoided; however, they can be minimized. The best way to accomplish this is through careful selection of your architect/engineers and contractor. You don't want an architect with the reputation of never completing his design work any more than you would want a contractor with the reputation of being a claims expert. Another way to minimize change orders is to have the best possible set of construction documents when the project goes to contract. Regardless of whether the construction work is to be awarded through negotiation or lump sum bid, the quality of the price is determined by the completeness of the construction documents. Quality of price does not necessarily mean lowest and cheapest price. It's easy for a developer to obtain low prices on incomplete documents, but chances are he will pay for it before the project is complete. The scope of work is not adequately detailed. Items changed or added later can easily be argued as being additions to the work. The focus should always be on the final price for the completed project and that can be best prepared from well prepared construction documents.

Control of the process does not end with the completion of the design effort and the start of construction. The design establishes the scope of work and definition and quality standards for the work and it also establishes the cost of construction. The management of the construction phase demands every bit as much attention as that of the design phase, because here again is the opportunity for the budget and schedule to go astray. The developer has a lump sum or guaranteed maximum construction contract. Many of his risks have been transferred to the contractor, but not all of them. The failure to properly manage or administer the construction phase can result in time delays and claims for additional costs.

In the construction phase, the developer, architect/engineers, and contractor are in their more traditional roles. The architect/engineers are responsible for design related services and the contractor for the delivery of the physical construction services. The architect/engineer's services during the construction phase have traditionally been:

- Contract Administration
- Shop Drawings and Submittal Review
- Construction Observation
- Monitoring the Schedule
- Cost Accounting Review and Approval of Progress Payments
- Review of Change Proposals and Issuance of Change Orders
- Preparation of Additional Documents as Required

This has all changed over the last ten or fifteen years and while the list of services may sound the same, they are actually not. For example, the architect's contract for construction related services calls for shop drawings and submittal review — but says nothing about approval or if it does, it is highly qualified. It calls for construction observation not construction inspection. Because of the increase in errors and omission claims against design firms, they have made a strong effort to minimize the potential of those claims by limiting certain responsibilities through contract language. The developer needs to recognize this and adjust his organization and approach to the construction phase to deal with it.

We have already talked about the typical causes of change orders relating to the design and the construction documents. During the construction phase, the lack of timely decisions and the handling of shop drawings and submittals are causes that most often result in change order requests and claims.

The developer must insure that both his own organization and that of the architect/engineer are adequate and are prepared to make decisions and to handle shop drawings and submittals in a timely manner so as not to prevent the orderly process of work.

It is desirable to have a full time designer and developer representative at the project site; however, only large projects can support the cost of this level of staffing. Nevertheless, numerous decisions must be made by the Owner and Architect. This charges the construction team with developing the organization structure and procedures to insure that it is accomplished. It is foolish to believe that regular and frequent project site visits by representatives of the developer and designers are not important to the success of the construction operations.

KEYPOINTS

The contractor's responsibility is to complete the construction for an agreed upon cost and within an established time period. The most critical asset for performance is the quality of the personnel assigned to the project. This is the reason that we strongly recommend the developer review the capability and experience of the contractor's proposed personnel before making a contractor selection. This should be done regardless of the approach to construction services delivery. The quality and number of personnel will depend on the size and complexity of the project; however, all the senior staff from project management to superintendent should be evaluated.

It is obvious that a developer needs to concentrate on a number of areas in managing the development process. The keys to realizing the most for the construction dollar are the people within a developer's organization who have responsibility for the design and construction process, the selection of the most appropriate construction delivery method, and an objective approach to the evaluation of the contractor's qualifications.

Lawrence A. Wilson is president and chief operating officer of HCB Contractors and is chairman and president of The Beck Company. HCB Contractors is one of the nation's largest general contractors with successfully completed commercial building projects in virtually every American city. HCB Contractors has regional offices in Atlanta, Los Angeles, and Houston, with its headquarters in Dallas. HCB's experience includes the construction of more than 100,000,000 square feet of class A high-rise office buildings and more than 20,000 hotel rooms.

Kenneth A. Shearer

MANAGING
REAL ESTATE PROPERTY

A discussion of owning and operating costs really begins with the tenant. The tenant is the ultimate consumer of the building services which create the operating costs.

We will be describing the control of these costs by looking first at the tenant and the conditions of the lease. In essence, you get what you pay for, but you must be knowledgeable about the benefits offered and received.

Then, we will discuss the organization and procedures required to begin management of a new property.

Finally, we will use a "case study" approach to buying a building and making various management policy changes to increase its financial performance.

THE LEASE

When discussing the cost of leasing space in a building, the cost is invariably reduced to "cost per square foot." The only problem is that the area can be defined differently depending upon how it is calculated.

For example, there is usable area (which is what the name implies) and rentable area, which varies. Rentable area is the usable area plus a pro rata share of the common use area used for public space and the space used for air conditioning and utilities. The BOMA (Building Owners and Managers Association) method of measurement measures space from the window line to the core for full floors, plus any air conditioning equipment rooms on the floor. In the case of split (multi-tenant) floors, the measurement is to the public hall walls and the halls and air conditioning room are apportioned on the basis of percentage of floor occupancy. Local real estate board measurements may apportion central mechanical rooms located elsewhere in the building plus shaft areas containing ducts or utilities to both full and part floor tenants. The difference between the usable and rentable area is called "the loss factor." Thus, when large areas are appor-tioned as part of rentable area, the effect is to increase the rentable area and the loss factor.

In marketing the space, it is essential to know the method by which the competing buildings' rentable areas are determined so that the advantages of your building's loss factor and actual rent can be emphasized. You must be aware of what tenant allowance or "work-letter" is being offered. The workletter, which defines the construction improvements which will be provided to the tenant, must be competitive. You must be able to define the differences between the offerings. In markets, such as New York, where local occupancy taxes exist, the tendency is to provide either cash allowances or workletter construction. Since the workletter cost including financing charges must be built into the rent over the term of the lease, it would be subject to such a tax. Reduction of this tax by having the tenant perform its own construction reduces the cost to the tenant.

Structure

The allowable floor loading in a building, the sum of "dead" and "live" loads, is of particular interest to tenants with large computer data centers or a need for large file areas. The ability to accommodate such tenants without supplementary support measures is a definite advantage.

Acoustics

The acoustical qualities of the building area are an important factor. Sound levels can be reduced if the building has been designed with adequate sound attenuation in the form of sound traps in ductwork, vibration isolation on mechanical equipment, and the treatment of partitions above the ceiling line to isolate noise from one space to the adjacent space.

Building Utilities

Building utilities (services) provided to tenants are often not given enough emphasis when comparisons are made with other buildings. The hours of operation for air conditioning in a commercial office building are normally from 8:00 a.m. to 6:00 p.m. from Monday through Friday. Whenever a tenant wishes to work at hours other than these standard hours, the tenant will incur charges for the provision of overtime air conditioning. The cost for these hours can be high for tenants such as accountants or attorneys and can sometimes be re-duced through the use of supplemental air conditioning units installed in the tenant's premises.

How much this costs depends upon what consideration has been given to designing a flexible air conditioning system. In some buildings it is necessary to turn on half of the building systems in order to provide air conditioning for any tenant. Costs for this type of system can be $200 per hour or greater in cities like New York. Buildings with smaller zones or individual air conditioning systems for each floor can provide much more competitive "overtime" heating and air-conditioning rates.

The cost of relamping the premises can be a significant cost to a large tenant. Relamping can be handled either as a building service or as a tenant charge.

Cleaning

The cleaning specification can vary significantly from building to building. The specification should be clear and very definitive. To describe cleaning as equal to that of a "first class office building" in a particular city is not too meaningful. The lease cleaning provision which clearly describes each function and the frequency is sure to result in a better relationship with the tenant, and allows the owner to provide the intended service.

Elevators

The elevator design in a building is most important. Everyone can think of a particular building in which the wait for an elevator seems to be interminable. This happens because the number of elevators is insufficient or the programming is incorrect for the type of use. For example, if a restaurant or cafeteria in an upper story creates a traffic pattern that is contrary to the normal building flow at a particular time of the day, this can be observed in other buildings and compared to your building through the judicious use of a stop watch.

Elevator speeds become important only if the building is tall enough to have long blind shafts for the express portion of the travel; however, floor to floor timing in any building is important. It is important to know if restrictions are placed on the use of elevators or if charges for overtime use are excessive.

Air Conditioning and Heating

Air conditioning and heating are *key* factors to a tenant. The types of controls are important from the point of view of flexibility. Air conditioning systems for office buildings are typically divided into a perimeter zone to meet varying exterior conditions, and an interior zone to handle what is normally a continuous cooling load. The subdivision of these zones into smaller areas through the use of therm-ostats in combination with valves or dampers is what creates additional flexibility for a tenant. The zones can then be assigned to each private office, if necessary. Perimeter systems using fan coil or induction units typically have a "building standard" of a number of units per bay with a thermostat for a number of bays. Additional therm-ostats and valves increases the number of control points and reduces the length of exterior wall per control. In the interior zone, mixing boxes or variable air volume controls in the ductwork subdivide the area served. Each of these devices has a thermostat in the controlled area. The cost of adding these devices is important and in some instances may make the cost of modifying an inflexible system very expensive. A comparison can be made of comparable buildings on the basis of guaranteed interior temperature and humidity when the exterior temperature and humidity, persons per square foot and total watts per square foot do not exceed given limits.

Power

The type of electrical system in your building is also important. How much power is installed in the risers serving the floor? Four to 6 watts per square foot of usable area is typical, allowing for a distribution of 3 to 5 watts per square foot on the floor. The number of lighting fixtures per square foot and the desk lighting level in foot candles are easily compared.

A statement of kilovolt amperes (KVA) per floor is used to indicate total power available which can be used for lighting, power, and any special electrical requirements. If the power available is inadequate, expensive reinforcing of the risers may be required. Tenants usually have to pay for this additional cost.

It is useful to know how comparable buildings are charging for electricity. Is it a fixed amount per square foot that is escalated for increased cost as rates change or when additional electrical equipment is added? Is it metered directly by the local utility, or is it submetered by the Landlord? If it's an escalatable fixed charge per square foot, how are these charges increased? Is it done by surveying the premises to estimate the consumption? If this is so, or if the use is submetered by the Landlord, what rate is used? It could be charged for on the same rate that the Landlord is purchasing power, it could be the average cost per KWHR paid by the Landlord, or it could be the rate that the utility would use if the tenant was purchasing power directly.

The most beneficial rate would be the average cost paid by the landlord. This would provide the benefit of the decreased cost of bulk purchasing power. The next most beneficial would depend upon the utility rate structure of the particular utility. Some utilities provide a better rate for large individual users than for users who redistribute. If this were so, then the tenant could utilize the rate at which he would purchase power directly. Otherwise, the rate at which the Landlord purchases power directly could be used. This is least beneficial if the utility charges the higher redistribution rate because each tenant's consumption is calculated by the landlord at the top end of the rate and no bulk purchasing benefit at the lower end of the rate is passed on to the tenant.

Life Safety

More and more tenants are becoming conscious of fire hazards in office buildings. The difference in life safety systems can transcend cost differences in the selection of a building in which to lease space. All buildings, as a minimum, should meet local code requirements. Exceeding these requirements is often necessary to provide a safe environment in which to work.

A sprinkler system is the most recognizable safety feature. This system can be combined with smoke detectors and a good communication system audible in all areas of the building. Being able to inform occupants in an emergency is crucial. Different localities have different requirements. They may require sprinklering, smoke detection, compartmentation of tenant space into specific maximum areas, smoke exhaust systems and stair pressurization. Emergency generators to provide emergency lighting and permit the movement of elevators are frequently required in new buildings.

Any responsible landlord will develop an emergency evacuation manual whether it is a local requirement or not and will perform evacuation drills for tenants.

Escalation Clauses

Escalation of operating cost clauses fall into two categories. The first is a pass through of actual increased operating costs when they exceed an established base. If the base is not artifically low and the pass through costs are not inflated, this is the most fair type of clause. It is difficult to audit these operating costs and Certified Public Accountants generally do not certify their authenticity.

The second type of clause is based upon an index and this type can be further subdivided into categories dependent upon the particular index used. The first index is the Consumer Price Index "CPI." Since this index is based upon many costs which do not pertain to operating a building, this index is often illogical to use. As a result (in order to satisfy tenants' objections), it is usually a negotiable item and its application is usually in the form of "— % of the CPI." An older index is "the porters' wage index." This is based upon the premise that operating costs increase at the same rate as porters' wages. This was true prior to energy cost increases in the last 15 years, because the greatest cost component was labor. If porters' wages increased one percent, then operating costs were assumed to have increased one percent. If the operating cost was $3.00 per square foot, then the rent would increase 3¢ per square foot for each percentage increase in porters' wages. The variations of this clause are many. For example, porters' wages may be defined as including benefits plus the hourly rate. The hourly rate may be defined as actual hours worked instead of hours paid. This method takes the annual wages plus benefits and is divided by the total hours in a year (2080) less vacations, sick days, holidays, etc. This deduction can reduce the annual hours considerably and thereby increase the labor cost per hour. It also compensates for any increase in vacation, holiday, or other costs which reduce annual productivity. the porter wage index has another variation which states that for each *cent* of increase in the porters' hourly rate, the rent will increase by an identical number of cents per square foot. Needless to say, this increase has no relationship to the building operating costs and results in an expensive escalation clause.

All of these index clauses were intended to reduce the time required to authenticate actual operating costs and resultant delays in collecting escalation from the tenant, and they may also be used in conjunction with a separate escalation for changes in electrical energy or rate changes. When this is done, the energy used for the base building is separated from the calculation. Thus, base building electricity is included in the index. Tenant electricty is separate.

If a pass through escalation clause is used, you often will be able to demonstrate to a potential client that your building is more energy efficient, and therefore, less expensive overall. Over the term of the lease in your building, substantial savings would accrue to the tenant. For example, if your building has been properly insulated and made energy efficient through the use of efficient lighting and energy management systems, these savings can be quantified and a favorable comparison can be made.

Building Management's Attitude and Responsiveness

The attitude of the building management must be analyzed. Some owners are very concerned about how the building is maintained and that tenants be satisfied to the maximum extent possible. Owners who historically hold buildings for long periods of time are usually more responsive to tenant requirements and generally are more likely to renew existing leases.

Security

The quality of security in different buildings varies considerably from virtually no security to identification of all persons entering a building. Unless a high level of security is maintained throughout the building during unoccupied time periods, incidents will occur which will result in tenant dissatisfaction.

Amenities

Building amenities must be emphasized. Parking for tenants and visitors must be adequate and available at a reasonable cost. Many recent buildings have not leased, because the brokerage community is aware of parking inadequacies.

The proximity of shopping, restaurants, clubs, theaters, and banks, either near or within the building must be emphasized. Mass transit, if available in the immediate area, is also a very desirable amenity.

Exterior Appearance

Last, but not least, is the consideration of the exterior of the building. Since curb appeal is a basic requirement to attract tenants, particular attention must be paid to landscaping, exterior finishes, and parking lot lighting. Good maintenance of these elements is critical. It makes no sense to spend time researching all of the above benefits described, and attracting a tenant to view the premises, only to have the tenant turned off before the space for lease is even viewed.

All of the above described features or "product facts" should be correlated and made part of a leasing brochure so that everything is in one convenient place. Remember that brochures do not lease buildings, but when they are used in conjunction with a good presentation by a knowledgeable person a successful leasing program is very likely to be the result!

START-UP AND PROPERTY MANAGEMENT

When a commercial office building is substantially completed, it is turned over to property management people for operation. Hopefully, sufficient time is allocated prior to tenant occupancy for the operating people to become familiar with the building systems and to participate in the "punch listing" of the building. Punch listing consists of listing all the defects or omissions that must be corrected in order for the contractor to comply with the terms of the construction contract to produce a functional finished product.

The time when a building manager should be in place at the building will vary depending on the size and complexity of the building. Sometimes, it is necessary to have a person in place during the steel erection phase of construction. Sometimes, the chief engineer should be there first; but in any event, either a chief engineer or building manager should be in place at least three months prior to the completion of construction.

Typically, the operating people familiarize themselves with the design of the mechanical systems, observe the installation of the mechanical and electrical equipment and participate in the final testing and start-up. One of the most important requirements is to document the location of piping, valves, coils, etc. prior to their enclosure by construction materials and finishes. These items should be photographed and then included in the building operating manual. The preparation of the building operating manual should begin as early as possible to complete the initial draft prior to the occupancy of the building.

The manual esentially is divided into three parts: administrative procedures, emergency procedures, and operating procedures. The manual would include:

1. Administrative Procedures
   a. General Building Information
   b. File Systems
   c. Personnel Procedures (Job descriptions, employment forms, etc.)
   d. Employment Procedures
   e. Procurement Procedures
   f. Budget Procedures (Definition, worksheet forms)
   g. Insurance Procedures (Claim forms, Contractors, Tenants)
   h. Tenant Procedures (Alterations, service requests, sundry billings)
   i. Miscellaneous Procedures

2. *Mechanical Procedures*

a. Equipment Schedules
b. Preventive Maintenance Program
c. Operational Procedures
d. Elevator Maintenance

3. *Emergency Procedures*

a. Fire Plan (Evacuation and alarms)
b. Bomb Threat
c. Inclement Weather (Hurricanes, dust storms, etc.)
d. Earthquakes
e. Power Blackouts
f. Glass Breakage
g. Illness or Accident
h. Flood

If a building is opened properly with the correct number and type of staff, training, and with procedures developed to produce an efficient operation, this will set the tone for the operation of the building for many years. If the buiding is opened poorly, then, of course, the reverse is true. For example, if the building is overstaffed, particularly in an area where unions are involved, it becomes very difficult and sometimes virtually impossible to reduce the staff to the level that it should have been.

How do you ensure that the building will be operated properly during the start-up period? The answer is — by developing a management plan. When starting up a new building or accepting the transfer of management of an existing building, it is not possible to have enough experience with this particular building to establish a final management plan. Therefore, an *interim* management plan should be developed until the occupancy of the building and the experienced gained in the operation is sufficient to establish a management plan. We have found these subjects to be key elements of a good interim management plan:

• Introduction — Management objectives
• Building Manual — Assembly of data
• Training and Organization — Objectives and methods
• Project Director — Identification and responsibilities
• Operations Manager — Identification and responsibilities
• Chief Engineer — Identification and responsibilities

The following is an example of such a plan:

INTERIM MANAGEMENT PLAN EXAMPLE

The objectives which are set forth in this Interim Management Plan are to be accomplished within the first three months of the management of the property. They are designed to meet the competitive market, achieve the financial goals for the property, and obtain the full engineered life of the structure and equipment.

In order to effectively manage real property, goals must be established to provide benchmarks by which performance is measured. This Plan defines the initial goals.

The scope of the plan includes budget analysis, review of administrative procedures, evaluation of staff, and review of maintenance procedures.

Building Operation Manual

The best way of assuring the establishment and continuation of efficient building operation is to eliminate oral tradition as a method of conveying information. All information pertinent to the administrative and mechanical operation of a building is reduced to a simple written form, which serves as a manual of operation.

Labor

(This section lists the staff required for the operation of the building for the next three months, taking into account the anticipated level of occupancy.)

Training

The objectives for personnel training will be as follows:

1. Utilize professional organizations such as Building Owners and Managers Association (BOMA) and Institute of Real Estate Management (IREM) educational courses to improve technical and management skills.
2. Utilize in-house training to improve technical and operating skill of the mechanical staff.
3. Improve self-motivation of staff through recognition. Employees will be interviewed twice each year to determine their job satisfaction, level of motivation and response to training programs.
4. Take advantage of local seminars and schools provided by vendors of mechanical equipment to improve operating skills of staff.
5. Establish salary range for different staff levels.

Organization

During the interim period, the owner or managing agent will supplement the on-site personnel. This is done to bring their experience into operation and establish procedures as quickly as possible.

Communication will be a prime factor in the success of this transition. A diagram includes the preferred lines of communication.

The supplemental staff will concentrate their efforts in four major areas: Building Administration, Accounting, Engineering, and Base Building Construction. "Base" Building Construction is that construction associated with the building and the mechanical/electrical systems which are not associated with "tenant improvement" construction.

Project Director

For the interim period, the project will be supervised by (name of staff member). Communication regarding this project and building operations will be the sole responsibility of the Project Director.

See *Figure 1* (page 187) for Management Organizational Chart for this interim period.

Emergency Procedures

- Emergency Manual — Tenants
    Fire
    Bomb Threats
    Severe Weather
    Blackouts
    Miscellaneous
- Emergency Manual — Employees
    Fire
    Bomb Threats
    Severe Weather
    Blackouts
    Miscellaneous
    Flooding
    Oil Spill
    Gas Leaks
    Elevators
- Fire Protection During Tenant Improvements
    Name person responsible for enforcing compliance by tenant improvement contractor
    Inspection schedule and log
    Fire extinguishers:
        Quantity
        Types
        Locations
    Name person responsible for enforcing compliance with federal and local fire codes and record keeping for:
        Type
        Location

　　　　　Inspection
　　　　　Recycling used extinguishers
　　　　Test schedule and log for standpipe building sprinkler
　　　　system.
　　• Security
　　　　　Interface with Building Security staff for key control.
　　　　　Security of mechanical, electrical and telephone equipment
　　　　　rooms.

Administration

　　• Purchase Order Procedures
　　　　　P. O. Log
　　　　　Acceptance and delivery tickets
　　　　　Approval of invoices
　　　　　Payment
　　• Budget
　　　　　Reconstruct present budget in agent's or new owner's format
　　　　　Verify costs
　　• Recap all annual purchase orders
　　　　　Perform contract abstracts in accordance with *Figure 2*
　　• Office Procedures
　　　　　Tenant and lease files
　　　　　Names of important representatives of tenants
　　　　　Directory Board Listings
　　　　　Tenant Signs
　　　　　Work Order System
　　　　　Preventive Maintenance System
　　　　　Complaint Log, Security Log, Contractors' Log, Cleaning
　　　　　Log
　　　　　Purchase Order System
　　　　　Payment Procedure
　　　　　Emergency Plans
　　• Personnel
　　　　　Evaluation Procedure
　　　　　Vacation
　　　　　Uniforms
　　　　　Sickness
　　　　　Hiring
　　　　　Terminating
　　• Energy Consumption Records
　　• Contract Files For:
　　　　　Cleaning
　　　　　Security
　　　　　Elevator
　　　　　Chemical treatment (cooling tower)
　　　　　Window washing
　　　　　Centrifugal chillers (maintenance contractor)
　　　　　Piped-in music

        Plant maintenance
        Building automation system
        Building HVAC control system
        Trash Removal
        Fire protection system
        Emergency generator
        Switch gear maintenance

- Building Passes
    List of building employees and type of identification issued
- Signage rules and directory board use.
- Forms for periodic reports to owner
- Lists of insurance agent, accountants, and other consultants
- Building Rules and Regulations
    Insure all employees are familiar with rules for:
        Tenants
        Lobby area
        Loading dock area
- Reporting System for Parking Lot Operators
- Overtime HVAC Charges
    Develop plan for tenant request for after hours services
- Building Inventory
    Lobby furniture
    Restroom furniture
    Lobby ashtrays
    Trash receptacles
    Maintenance and engineering office furniture
    Special equipment
- Tenant Improvement Plan
    Procedures for establishing line of communication for the following:
        Scheduling and acceptance of tenant improvements
    Tenant Move-In
        Coordination of move-in with tenant and movers
        Coordination of:
            Telephones
            Security
            Elevator use
            Mail
            Trash removal
            Keys (Access Cards)
            Cleaning
            Directory Listing
- Janitorial
    Tenant After Move-In
        Follow-up for such items as Tenant space clean up (special)
    Restroom cleaning
    Restroom supplies

Tenant complaints
- Operations Newsletter
- Interface with Leasing Group
- Develop Management's Office Space

Construction Manager

The coordination of the acceptance of the base building construction will be the responsiblity of the building manager with the aid of one of the operation secretaries.

The areas of responsibility are:

Acceptance of Base Building floors
Acceptance of Base Building equipment. (Coordinate this with Engineering section.)
Obtain status of all utilities
Who is paying bills?
In whose names are utility services listed?
When will services be in name of owner?
(Initially, these services may be in the name of a construction company and are transferred to an operating corporation at some point when permanent financing or acceptance for operating is achieved.)

Chief Engineer

The responsibility for implementing engineering procedures is a joint effort between the chief engineer and the building manager.

The following items are to be reviewed/developed and directions given to fully indoctrinate each engineer to ensure implementation:

Tool/Equipment Inventory and Procedures
Preventive Maintenance Systems
Work Order System
Interview and evaluate engineering staff including job
    description, work schedule, training, and
    operating procedures.
Make recommendations regarding communication system for
    engineering staff.
Engineers conduct/appearance while working in building

Each of the three disciplines, "operation," "engineering," and "construction," are to develop an interim management plan establishing dates to accomplish the tasks outlined above.

Figure 1   INTERIM ORGANIZATIONAL CHART

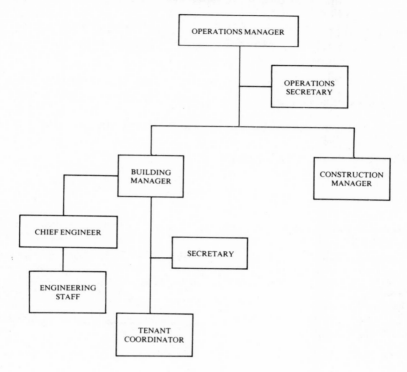

Figure 2

CONTRACT ABSTRACT

1. Contract/Vendor $ _____
2. Service Provided: $ _____
3. Cost/Year: $ _____
4. Billing (Monthly, Quarterly, etc.): $ _____
5. Billing Cost: $ _____
6. Term/Effective Date: _____
7. Cancellation: _____
8. Comments/Unusual Terms: _____

_____

9. Purchase order No./Date: _____
   Vendor Address: _____
   Telephone: _____
   Contact: _____

The Operation and Engineering Managers are to develop a Management Plan outlining objectives and goals for the permanent operating staff during the first twelve months. This would be for the next twelve months for a building which is operating, and the first 12 months for a new building.

MANAGING THE "TURNAROUND"

Previously, we have discussed issues pertaining to leasing and procedures for beginning service for a new building or the takeover of an existing building.

PROJECTED INCOME AND EXPENSES — 1983 to 1991

YEARS OF PROJECTION	1983*	1984	1985
Base Rental Income[1]	$1,363,675	$2,157,550	$2,181,650
Escalations			
Real Estate Taxes[2]	29,455	116,555	260,155
Operating[3]	0	2,125	9,580
CPI and Porters' Wages[4]	16,320	65,960	140,450
Total Rental Income:	1,409,450	2,342,130	2,591,835
Less Vacancy (3%)[5]	42,280	70,265	77,755
Effective Gross Income	1,367,170	2,271,865	2,514,080
Operating Expense[6]	302,130	435,070	469,875
Real Estate Taxes[7]	203,540	371,170	478,475
Total Operating Expenses:	505,670	806,240	948,350
Net Operating Income:	861,500	1,465,625	1,565,730
Less Commissions[8]	260,520	0	0
CASH FLOW:	$ 600,980	$1,465,625	$1,565,730
CASH-ON-CASH**	5.96%	10.90%	11.64%

*Nine months of 1983
**Annualized Return
1 $25.00 psf has been employed and escalated at the rate of 5% a year.
2 Tax escalations — Every tenant pays its proportionate share of increases in the Real Estate Taxes over their particular base year.
3 Operating Escalations were computed as follows:
  (a) As the lease abstracts outlined.
  (b) As the leases expire 1¢ for 1¢ porters' wage with fringe benefits.
4 As the lease abstracts outlined.
5 Computed as 3% of the gross income.

The following case study illustrates the traditional real estate "turn-around," in which an acquisition of a building was based on the upside potential of changes in the ownership strategy. The pro forma which follows will give you a feel for the owning and occupancy costs.

A Case Study of the Purchase and Operation of an Urban Office Building

In 1982, an offshore group wished to purchase a commercial office building preferably in a Southern California urban area. Submittals were requested from various real estate companies and

1986	1987	1988	1989	1990	1991
$2,188,650	$2,264,065	$2,271,065	$2,278,065	$2,355,815	$2,362,815
382,315	402,260	447,640	479,380	487,280	521,625
28,165	43,535	72,040	102,300	126,370	162,205
207,770	212,000	298,065	381,740	471,485	572,650
2,806,900	2,921,860	3,088,810	3,241,485	3,440,950	3,619,295
84,205	87,655	92,660	97,240	103,230	108,575
2,722,695	2,834,205	2,996,150	3,144,245	3,337,720	3,510,720
507,465	548,060	591,910	639,260	690,400	745,630
593,790	717,620	746,330	776,160	807,180	839,455
1,101,255	1,265,680	1,388,240	1,415,420	1,497,580	1,585,085
1,621,440	1,568,525	1,67,910	1,728,825	1,840,140	1,925,635
0	74,260	0	0	9,520	0
$1,621,440	$1,494,265	$1,607,910	$1,728,825	$1,830,620	$1,925,635
12.06%	11.11%	11.95%	12.85%	13.61%	14.32%

6 Operating expenses were increased at the rate of 8% a year.
7 Real Estate Taxes were increased at the rate of 4% a year.
8 Commissions have been calculated as 28.25% of the first year's rent at each lease turnover. This assumes an 8½ year lease.

INCOME DATA PRESENTED HEREIN, WHILE BASED UPON HISTORICAL FIGURES CANNOT BE CONSIDERED ACCURATE, FOR THEY ARE
FICTICIOUS CALCULATIONS UTILIZED STRICTLY FOR PURPOSES OF PRO FORMA PROJECTIONS AND ANALYSIS.

after they were analyzed, a building was selected.

The building was approximately 60 years old and was located in a prime downtown area. The building was typical for the period, brick exterior with double hung sash and had been minimally maintained over the past 20 years or so. The building contained 15 stories and a penthouse and contained 73,500 square feet. The building was located adjacent to similar types of buildings. Research indicated that adjacent leases expired by 1991. This indicated that plans were being made by the adjacent owners to demolish the buildings and redevelop the block in 1991. As a result, the pro forma was projected for eight years on the assumption that if leases were limited to this period, the purchasers

PROJECTED RENT ROLL — 1983 TO 1993

LOCATION	S.F.	1983**	1984	1985
Estimated Rent/sf		$25.00	$26.25	$27.50
Bsmt./Ground/Mezz		268,750	428,500	434,500
2F	1700	33,600	44,800	44,800
2R	3000	17,625	23,500	35,000
3	4700	45,000	95,600	101,200
4	4700	50,525*	101,050	101,050
5	4700	58,750*	117,500	117,500
6	4400	90,000	120,000	120,000
7	4400	85,800	114,400	114,400
8	4400	55,000*	110,000	110,000
9	4400	55,000*	110,000	110,000
10	4400	55,000*	110,000	110,000
11	4000	50,000*	100,000	100,000
12	4000	78,000	104,000	104,000
13	4000	62,500	110,000	110,000
14	4000	53,000*	106,000	106,000
15 and Penthouse	5600	75,600*	151,200	151,200
Rental Income 1st 3 Months		53,275		
Annex Building 2-6 Floors	9750	158,250	211,000	211,000
TOTAL INCOME		1,363,675	2,157,550	2,181,650

*Denotes the year in which lease expires.
**Nine Months of 1983

would be in a position to either buy out the adjacent owners and develop the block themselves, sell to the adjacent owners, or participate in a joint venture as a partner.

In other words, they had future options available beyond just increasing the net operating income of the property.

The building was occupied by a large number of small tenants and it was decided that instead of just obtaining a nominal incremental increase from existing tenants that entire floors would be vacated, renovated and re-leased as prime space at prime rentals. All leases were to expire in 1991 to provide the owner with the above described options at that time.

The projections show a rate of return of 5.96% in 1983 increas-

1986	1987	1988	1989	1990	1991
$29.00	$30.50	$32.00	$33.50	$35.25	$37.00
442,500	449,500	456,500	463,500	470,500	477,500*
44,800	44,800	44,800	44,800	44,800	44,800*
35,000	35,000	35,000	35,000*	105,750	105,750*
101,200	105,600	105,600	105,600	105,600	105,600*
101,050	101,050	101,050	101,050	101,050	101,050*
117,500	117,500	117,500	117,500	117,500	117,500*
120,000*	134,200	134,200	134,200	134,200	134,200*
114,400	114,400	114,400	114,400	114,400	114,400*
110,000	110,000	110,000	110,000	110,000	110,000*
110,000	110,000	110,000	110,000	110,000	110,000*
110,000	110,000	110,000	110,000	110,000	110,000*
100,000	100,000	100,000	100,000	100,000	100,000*
104,000	104,000	104,000	104,000	104,000	104,000*
110,000	110,000	110,000	110,000	110,000	110,000*
106,000	106,000	106,000	106,000	106,000	106,000*
151,200	151,200	151,200	151,200	151,200	151,200*

| 211,000* | 260,815 | 260,815 | 260,815 | 260,815 | 260,815 |
| $2,188,650 | $2,264,065 | $2,271,065 | $2,278,065 | $2,355,815 | $2,362,815 |

ing to 14.32% in 1991. The average rent when the building was purchasd was $14.00 per square foot maximum and was increased to $25.00 per square foot after capital improvements were to be made in 1983, thereafter projected to escalate 5% per year in the pro forma.

SUMMARY

Producing a profit in real estate property management requires a good understanding of the income side (negotiating leases) and the expense side (controlling costs) of the ledger.

Negotiating leases is the *key* to generating strong cash flow, while cost control of expenses involves purchasing and management skills. Property managers must have a "bottom line" orientation. Every dollar counts. Yet, *attentive service to the tenants* must be thoughtfully and conscientiously maintained.

Ken Shearer is executive vice-president and national director of property management for Cushman & Wakefield. Cushman & Wakefield, with more than 65 years of experience, has real estate brokerage and property management offices in more than 46 major markets throughout the United States. At the present time, Cushman & Wakefield is managing more than 70 million square feet of commercial, office, industrial, and retail space. Ken Shearer is a director of the New York Realty Advisory Board on Labor Relations, and has been active in New York City real estate for more than 30 years.

James S. Madden

WHEN TO SELL

When should you sell property? How long should you hold property? Are there specific principles one can apply?

While these questions are quite broad, reasonable answers exist that go beyond the equally general truism, "Buy low and sell high."

When buying or building, owners make a financial commitment to a property because it represents the best choice available at the time. The acquisition period is usually fairly short.

An owner does not expect to face circumstances that would create a comparable short time pressure to sell. Morerover, whether the prop-erty is meeting expectations or not, an owner often prefers dealing with the more relaxed responsibilities of managing a known entity, versus the pressures and anxieties of trying to evaluate and buy an unknown property. When you can sell at any time, what's the hurry about deciding When To Sell?

Two valid reasons for concern should be considered: First, the "success" of your investment is determined more by the results of its sale than its yearly operations; secondly, regardless of the property's performance, "unusual circumstances" may arise that make you want to sell, or even force you to sell, on unexpectedly short notice.

Real estate is not liquid. Selling income properties valued under $1 million takes four to eight months from listing to closing. Larger, unique, or problem properties can take much longer. Yet the terms, conditions, and value of a property's sale can change drastically over these relatively short periods. You cannot afford to wait and react to changes. You have to anticipate change, even though you are not sure exactly what the change will be.

While you cannot expect to sustain the intense focus that preceded your purchase of a property, you will need to re-examine regularly your decision to own. Look at selling this way: holding a property is a decision NOT to sell. What reasons, other than convenience, do you have for keeping a property?

Throughout this chapter, we will discuss various influences on your decision to sell, and give you some hypothetical examples that I hope will help you make informed decisions.

Deciding when to sell could be compared to solving a mystery: you must get the facts straight, such as what, why, how and when. Selling is also a question of motive — that is, identifying your goals and strategies.

SELL WHAT?

You probably should read the title to this section with the same inflection as that well-known phrase, "Say what?" In fact, the two questions could be confused, or even interchanged on many occasions. For example, you could be talking with a securities dealer when he asks you:

"Why not sell a partially guaranteed, convertible-debt security against a participating mortgage pool."

"Sell (say) what?"

In fact, because many, many components of a property can be sold, most texts describe real estate ownership as a "bundle of rights." That bundle constitutes one of the beauties of real estate, wholly apart from any physical attributes.

In lieu of an outright sale, rights most often sold include mineral rights, easement rights, development rights and air rights. In addition to the sale of all rights, sellers and buyers constantly devise ownership structures that create special interests in property.

For example, approaches range from the sale-leaseback and the sale-buyback, to a sale with participation, and even a sale with "pregnant" leaseback. Syndications' sales match certain benefits, generally tax benefits, with certain investors. Often several different classes of benefits will be sold for one property to attract a wider range of investors.

Extending even beyond these diverse sales options, Wall Street has devised some really esoteric real estate investments. With governmental support, Wall Street created and sold securities which are rights to the income from a pool of government-insured mortgages. This concept has been extended to privately-insured conventional mortgages, participating mortgages, and even some equities. The offerings usually involve at least 20 pounds of documents, and five to six-figure legal bills, but Wall Street investors have learned to love them. And they defy simple description. They were also the only way the real estate industry could tap national capital markets.

So what does all this mean? It means that you may be able to sell specific interests to real estate to meet your investment goals. You are not necessarily restricted to an outright sale.

Let us give you an example of a sale that was structured unconventionally. In 1975 I was working in the San Francisco office of an insurance company's real estate investment group. We were approached by advisors for a property company owned by a group of British pension funds. They made a proposal to invest jointly in some projects. While the shareholder funds were quite large, their foreign investment was limited at the time by British capital-export controls. Despite this, the advisors constantly received extremely interesting offers.

Our first transaction together involved a straight purchase of an office building. The second transaction was unusual, particularly for that time. We were approached by a member of a family which was the majority owner of Ghirardelli Square in San Francisco, the first "specialty shopping center" in the U.S. He was making a very discrete inquiry whether we were interested in the property. Of course, we were. A great concept in a great location.

In our first meeting, it quickly became apparent that the property *wasn't* for sale, at least not quite. In 1966 a small group of wealthy, civic-minded people bought Ghirardelli to save it from being torn down and replaced by highrise apartments. The buyers were not even sure what they could do with the property, but a talented group of architects and this dedicated and imaginative group of owners devised a plan for a shopping center anchored by restaurants. So it came to be.

I had always thought that Ghirardelli was as financially successful as it was architecturally pleasing. In reality, it had been a difficult investment. In 1975, six years after it opened to much acclaim, Ghirardelli was not worth as much as it cost, at least when evaluated strictly on an income-generating basis. The owners who had invested a lot of cash to develop and carry the property, had amassed as much cash equity as debt. It was not ready for a sale.

Yet there were some compelling reasons for the owners to get a purchase commitment. A major investor, though in good health, was over sixty. Advisors had pointed out that a death could force the estate to sell cheaply to pay estate taxes. The owners also believed Ghirardelli was, and would be, worth a lot more than could be realized in an outright sale, and they wanted to prove it.

Therefore, we began a lengthy process to determine how to buy Ghirardelli when they were ready to sell. After several months, we finally agreed on a purchase formula. The contract provided that the sale could be triggered by the Seller at any time, up to seven years in the future! The purchase price was calculated by capitalizing the future adjusted net operating income, as defined and audited, at a set rate to determine value. Of course, the term "income," was defined thoroughly, and specific guidelines and approval procedures were established for all leases that would extend beyond seven years.

This sale was an "extended earn-out," a very unusual transaction at the time. The parties had to share many rights of management, and had to have a formal agreement to arrive at the future basis of price.

The sale? It went through at the end of the seventh year in early 1983. The Sellers made a handsome profit, and the Buyers were equally pleased.

The most interesting aspect of this transaction was that initially what we were buying was not real estate, but future rights to real estate. The Sellers had enough time in which to earn their profit, while insuring a reasonable sale could be made if they were forced to sell early. They "sold" their right to sell to others, or to sell at whatever price the future market would dictate.

Today, the earn-out has become common, and is usually structured as a convertible mortgage. A lender, typically either a pension fund or an insurance company, makes a full loan for the option to convert the loan to an equity position 6 to 10 years in the future.

The convertible mortgage represents a good example of selling specific real estate rights to those that want some, but not all, of real estate's characteristics. Pension funds want yield plus inflation protection, but cannot use tax benefits. With a convertible mortgage, the developer retains the tax benefits, some of the appreciation before conversion, and a share of the residual. If the developer cannot use the tax benefits, he may, in turn, syndicate them to investors who can.

The point of these examples is to illustrate that you have many options to evaluate when deciding to sell. One should think creatively about exactly *what* there is to sell.

In spite of this discussion's focus, an outright sale is the easiest, quickest, and probably the most profitable option in most instances and for most properties. Creating special interest in your property incurs additional professional fees and transaction costs. Also, buyers generally like to control the properties they purchase, and to structure the sales of rights and interests to meet their own goals. However, special opportunities often become available, or other compelling reasons develop that warrant selling less than the whole pie.

WHY SELL?

You have gone through considerable effort building or buying this property. You own it. You have it leased. It is well-located in an attractive, growing area. Your property manager is top-notch and cheap — almost irreplaceable — and the property generates a pretty good cash flow. Why sell?

Compelling reasons exist even for selling productive, quality real estate. Some reasons are somewhat perverse, and some are beyond your control.

Real estate is just one of many investments in most investment portfolios. As times change, both the returns on, and the quality of, that portfolio change. Ownership goals also shift. For example, the following statements reveal a number of different reasons for selling:

- "He sold his building to raise money for business expansion."
- "The company announced a policy designed to re-deploy assets and reduce debt."
- "She announced that after the sale of her properties, she would spend more time in charitable activities and travel."
- "The partnership was selling some of its best properties to support the cash needs of its new developments."

As these examples illustrate, the reasons for selling often have little to do with the property's intrinsic worth. Changes in ownership goals really motivate sales.

Therefore, it becomes critically important to understand that your goals, not the property condition, are the most important trigger of the "Why Sell?" and "When to Sell?" decision.

Goals and Strategies

A simple answer to "When to Sell?" is: when you have met the goals you set at acquisition. Though this approach may seem practical, it probably isn't!

This simple answer doesn't work, because the goals you set for the property are really part of your strategy for meeting overall objectives. When you acquired the property, the mix of investments, opportunities, and capital plus your future outlook were different. The property met current criteria. But criteria invariably change over time.

While personal or corporate goals usually remain pretty stable, the strategies to achieve these goals change dramatically. For example, many developers' goals can be characterized in the following two sentences: 1) They want the highest possible financial rewards from their efforts; 2) They want to see, and have others see, what their efforts have produced.

The strategies a developer uses to achieve these goals change rapidly. One year he may be building for-sale housing, the next year he may make long term investments in apartments. Flexibility is the key because conditions change constantly.

The performance and prospects of a property also change constantly.

If we evaluate a sale simply by calculating the property's investment return, we only measure the mathematical return over the holding period. This single analysis will not tell us whether or not the sale met your objectives.

Please note the subtle but important distinction. The "optimum" ownership period for a property as measured by the financial return between two points in time, differs from the optimum period of ownership for an owner. Success comes from matching the two.

For example, suppose you own a property that you are sure will be worth much more next year when a neighboring development is completed. However, another special opportunity arises that you can only take advantage of if you sell the property now. Clearly, the optimum return on your property conflicts with other important goals. If your special opportunity is that Caribbean yacht you've always wanted, the choice may be obvious.

Before continuing, we need to make a special comment about the goals and strategies of partnerships. The changing strategies of the individual partners cause special problems, particularly in partnerships between developers and financial institutions. These partners are often matched at the outset, yet the forces affecting their strategies vary considerably.

Because decisions must be shared between these partners in different businesses, it becomes vitally important that they have a written business plan as part of their partnership agreement. It should specify the current market and financial conditions, the partners' goals for the project, and the forecasted financial results.

In most public-partnership syndications, investors agree on the goals in the beginning, and the syndicator tries to achieve them. The optimum return for the property's ownership period usually becomes most important.

Despite all the emphasis on the owners' goals, the expected return is one of the main reasons you purchased the property. Tracking the actual return over the ownership period tells you something about how your property performed.

Below we have developed an example of the financial returns of a typical property during the ownership period. It displays certain unique characteristics that influence the decision to sell.

Product Ownership Period

First, we need to make a distinction between property built or purchased for investment, and property built for sale.

Most experienced developers realize that it is becoming increasingly difficult to develop income property solely for investment. Lead times are longer, competition more intense, and equity requirements have increased substantially. You need a number of skilled, highly paid and motivated people to run a development company and this means you must keep an on-going inventory of projects. To complicate things further, Wall Street does not have much interest in providing equity for property companies; and lenders will not provide enough in all cases to cover project costs and overhead for future projects. Consequently, most developers who want to grow must become merchant builders. They build products to sell to the investor market.

While merchant builders have some flexibility in deciding when to sell a given project, they do not have that much when you consider their entire company's production. They must generate cash from sales on a regular basis, or else reduce their staff and other overhead.

With this impetus to sell, short-term planning becomes critically important. Long term forecasts are largely irrelevant. Selling is their key to survival.

While the total measured return on investment for any given project can be extremely high, the largest increment in value is created when taking a property from its undeveloped to developed state. Once developed, the returns fall into line with similar existing investments. Therefore, joint ventures, syndications, and pre-sales are likely to be attractive to investors. They also provide the merchant builder with greater flexibility on other projects which he may be building alone.

Now, we will focus on the long-term investor by creating a realistic example of a typical income property investment.

We are going to keep this example fairly simple, but true to the basic relationships that currently exist in many properties today. It was developed on a common computer spreadsheet program using the general format we have designed for analyzing any investment or development property.

First, we'll call our property "The Commercial Centre." It is a new office building, purchased shortly after it was built and leased. The property was purchased for $6.5 million, which equates to a 10% cap rate and a cost of about $93 per square foot.

The purchase was financed by a mortgage of $4,875,000 at a

rate of 13.5% payable over 30 years. The debt service is a tight 1.05 times. The equity was $2,015,000, which represented 31% of the purchase price.

For simplicity, we will also assume that the vacancy level remains constant, and that revenue and expenses rise at the same inflation rate of 5%. In addition, after the fifth year, we have indicated some additional capital costs for re-leasing and tenant improvements. These assumptions are summarized in *Table 1*.

By calculating the consequences of these income and purchase price assumptions over a 10 year time span, we arrive at the figures shown in *Table 2*. (Before the computer spreadsheet programs became readily available, I would tediously do this kind of analysis manually. My secretary and I would dread the thought of having to correct an error, or change an assumption an hour before making an investment committee presentation. Now the correction takes about nine seconds!)

Note that in the beginning the net income is negative, but that it grows steadily as the net operating income increases through inflation (or appreciation). The total interest expense also declines as more of each payment goes toward principal.

Table 1

THE COMMERCIAL CENTRE/ASSUMPTIONS
($ 000's)

Purchase Price

Purchase Allocation

Land	20%	$1,300
Building	75%	4,875
Other	5%	325
Total		$6,500

Sources of Funds

Loan	69%	4,485
Equity	31%	2,015
Total		$6,500

Purchase Data

Building Area	70,000 s.f.
Price/SF	$92.86
Average $/SF/Year Rent	$15.04
(Based on 5% Vacancy)	
Operating Expenses	$5.00/s.f.

Capital Improvements: 20% of space each year after fifth year @ $5.00/SF times the inflation rate

Capitalization Rate on Purchase and Sale	10%

Net Operating Income before Debt Service	10.04/s.f.
Inflation Rate all items	5%

The bottom of Table 2 lists two common measures of the annual return from a property: cash flow before and after-tax. These measures are shown both as their absolute amounts, and as a ratio of the initial equity. Like net income, they also increase over time as the operating income increases. The "Cash Flow A.T." starts higher than the "Cash Flow B.T.," however, the gap between them narrows. Then they cross over. This would occur even if there was zero inflation because with each extra dollar of before-tax cash flow, a steadily decreasing amount is added to the after-tax cash flow due to declining tax benefits. This is a clear example of diminishing return on income over time.

The graph in Figure 1 illustrates quite effectively this relationship between net income, cash flow before-tax, and cash flow after-tax. Between the fifth and sixth years you'll also observe two "crossover" points: a) Net income rises from a negative figure to a positive one; and b) the cash flow lines cross.

Figure 1

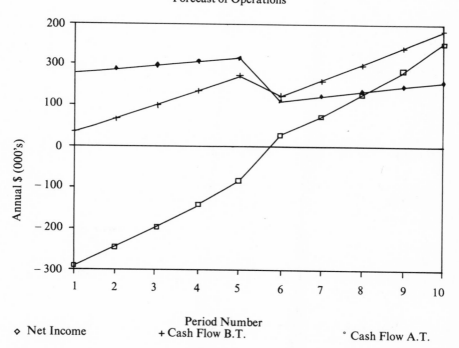

THE COMMERCIAL CENTRE

Forecast of Operations

◇ Net Income   + Cash Flow B.T.   ° Cash Flow A.T.

Table 2
THE COMMERCIAL CENTRE PRO FORMA
($000's)

Income Statement

	1	2	3
Net Revenue	1,000	1,050	1,103
– Operating Expenses 35%	(350)	(368)	(386)
Operating Income	650	683	717
– Depreciation	(336)	(336)	(336)
– Interest	(605)	(591)	(576)
Net Income (Loss)	(291)	(245)	(195)
Principal Repayments	(12)	(25)	(40)
Depreciation	336	336	336
Capital Cost Releasing	0	0	0
Cash Flow	34	66	100

Return On Equity
  Equity = 2,015

Return on Equity			
Before Tax	1.66%	3.29%	4.79%
Tax benefit of losses			
50.00%	145	122	98
Cash Flow	34	66	100
After-tax Cash Flow	179	188	198
Return on Equity	8.8%	9.35%	9.82%
After Tax			

Before we can come to any more general conclusions, we must examine some other measures of performance that include the value of property over time.

Schedules on the next table *(Table 3)* show depreciation of the building and personal property, loan amortization and interest costs, and a balance sheet by year.

We have included a balance sheet because it is the only way to really tell whether your figures add up. (Unfortunately, most cash flow projections, even "canned" computer programs, do not include them, nor can they be tailored to each property's unique characteristics.)

This balance sheet is very simple. It assumes there is no undistributed cash, and no accrual accounts. The "P&L" account is retained earnings: it is reduced by losses and cash flow before-tax, (which is assumed to be distributed), and increased by profits.

4	5	6	7	8	9	10
1,158	1,216	1,276	1,340	1,407	1,477	1,551
(405)	(425)	(447)	(469)	(492)	(517)	(543)
752	790	830	871	915	960	1,003
(336)	(336)	(289)	(307)	(327)	(348)	(370)
(559)	(539)	(516)	(490)	(460)	(425)	(386)
(142)	(84)	25	74	128	187	253
(58)	(78)	(101)	(127)	(157)	(191)	(230)
336	336	289	307	327	348	370
0	0	(89)	(94)	(98)	(103)	(109)
136	174	124	1,161	200	240	283
6.75%	8.62%	6.14%	7.99%	9.91%	11.93%	14.06%
71	42	(13)	(37)	(64)	(94)	(126)
136	174	124	161	200	240	283
207	216	111	124	136	147	157
10.27%	10.71%	5.52%	6.14%	6.74%	7.29%	7.79%

Table 3

THE COMMERCIAL CENTRE PRO FORMA
($ 000's)

BALANCE SHEET

Year:	0	1	2	3
Assets:				
Land	1,300	1,300	1,300	1,300
Buildings	4,875	4,875	4,875	4,875
– Accumulated Depreciation		(271)	(542)	(813)
Other	325	325	325	325
– Accumulated Depreciation		(65)	(130)	(195)
TOTAL ASSETS	6,500	6,164	5,829	5,493
Liabilities:				
Loan	4,485	4,473	4,448	4,408
Equity	2,015	2,015	2,015	2,015
P&L	0	(324)	(635)	(930)
TOTAL LIABILITIES	6,500	6,164	5,828	5,493

Subsidiary Schedules:

Building Depreciation: 18 years, straight line

Beginning		4,875	4,604	4,333
– Depreciation		(271)	(271)	(271)
ENDING		4,604	4,333	4,063

Other Depreciation: 5 years, straight line

Beginning		325	260	195
Additions		0	0	0
– Depreciation		(65)	(65)	(65)
ENDING		260	195	130

Loan Amortization Schedule:
  Loan Rate 13.50%   Coverage Ratio = 1.05 times
  # Months 360
  Annual Payment 616

Beginning Loan		4,485	4,473	4,448
– Amortization		(12)	(25)	(40)
ENDING		4,473	4,448	4,408
ANNUAL INTEREST		605	591	576

4	5	6	7	8	9	10
1,300	1,300	1,300	1,300	1,300	1,300	1,300
4,875	4,875	4,875	4,875	4,875	4,875	4,875
(1,083)	(1,354)	(1,625)	(1,896)	(2,167)	(2,438)	(2,708)
325	325	414	508	607	710	819
(260)	(325)	(343)	(379)	(436)	(513)	(612)
5,157	4,821	4,621	4,408	4,179	3,935	3,674
4,350	4,272	4,171	4,045	3,888	3,697	3,467
2,015	2,015	2,015	2,015	2,015	2,015	2,015
(1,208)	(1,466)	(1,565)	(1,652)	(1,724)	(1,777)	(1,808)
5,157	4,821	4,621	4,408	4,179	3,935	3,674
4,063	3,792	3,521	3,250	2,979	2,708	2,438
(271)	(271)	(271)	(271)	(271)	(271)	(271)
3,792	3,521	3,250	2,979	2,708	2,438	2,167
130	65	0	71	129	171	197
0	0	89	94	98	103	104
(65)	(65)	(18)	(37)	(56)	(77)	(99)
65	0	71	129	171	197	207
4,408	4,350	4,272	4,171	4,045	3,888	3,697
(58)	(78)	(101)	(127)	(157)	(191)	(230)
4,350	4,272	4,171	4,045	3,888	3,697	3,467
559	539	516	490	460	425	386

Table 4

THE COMMERCIAL CENTRE PRO FORMA

Estimated Sales Proceeds

	1	2	3	4
Cash Proceeds:				
Sale @ Cap Rate				
of 10.00%	6,500	6,825	7,166	7,525
– Commission and				
Closing 4.5%	(293)	(307)	(322)	(339)
Gross Proceeds	6,208	6,518	6,844	7,186
Loan Repayment	(4,473)	(4,448)	(4,408)	(4,350)
Net Proceeds				
Before-Tax	1,734	2,070	2,436	2,836
Taxes upon Sale:				
Sale @ Cap Rate				
of 10.00 %	6,500	6,825	7,166	7,525
– Commission and				
Closing 4.5%	(293)	(307)	(322)	(339)
Gross Proceeds	6,208	6,518	6,844	7,186
– Land Cost	(1,300)	(1,300)	(1,300)	(1,300)
– Building Basis	(4,604)	(4,333)	(4,063)	(3,792)
– Other Basis	(260)	(195)	(130)	(65)
Capital Gain	43	690	1,351	2,029
Capital Gains Tax				
On Taxpayer in a				
50% Tax-Bracket	(9)	(138)	(270)	(406)

Table 4 presents some very interesting calculations. This set of figures is calculated to evaluate the effects of sale "as-if" a sale oc-curred at the end of each year. The terms of sale are assumed to be the same as those of purchase: an all-cash sale at a 10% cap rate on the operating income.

The two calculations are similar to the annual cash flow measures discussed above: the proceeds of a sale are figured before and after-tax. Net Cash Proceeds is the sum of the purchase price less commissions, closing costs, and the loan balance. Next, the Capital Gain for the sale is calculated so that the amount of tax due from each sale can be estimated. Note that in both cases, the balance sheet figures are very handy as a source for the calculations.

Now, we have all the figures necessary to calculate the return over time.

5	6	7	8	9	10
7,901	8,296	8,711	9,146	9,603	10,084
(356)	(373)	(392)	(412)	(432)	(454)
7,545	7,923	8,319	8,735	9,171	9,630
(4,272)	(4,171)	(4,045)	(3,888)	(3,697)	(3,467)
3,273	3,751	4,274	4,847	5,475	6,163
7,901	8,296	8,711	9,146	9,603	10,084
(356)	(373)	(392)	(412)	(432)	(454)
7,545	7,923	8,319	8,735	9,171	9,630
(1,300)	(1,300)	(1,300)	(1,300)	(1,300)	(1,300)
(3,521)	(3,250)	(2,979)	(2,708)	(2,438)	(2,167)
(0)	(71)	(129)	(171)	(197)	(207)
2,724	3,301	3,911	4,555	5,237	5,956
(545)	(660)	(782)	(911)	(1,047)	(1,191)

The final page of figures, *Table 5,* recaps the annual figures, including the sale on an after-tax basis. The figures are then carried down in a format that allows the computer to figure the Internal Rate of Return (IRR) for each year.

The first IRR, calculated after one year, is negative because the transaction costs are not covered by the assumed appreciation over one year. Of course, we have all seen a property that is sold after one year for a huge gain, but, we don't need computers to figure out that kind of deal! Typically, the IRR grows rapidly for a couple of years and then begins to flatten out, much like the cash flow measures.

Another measure at the bottom of Table 5, the Return on Current Equity Value, is calculated by taking the Net Proceeds after tax compared to that year's cash flow After-tax. This measure shows a consistent decline over time.

Table 5

INTERNAL RATE OF RETURN

		1	2	3	4
Annual Cash Flow After-tax		179	188	198	207
Net Proceeds Before-tax		1,734	2,070	2,436	2,836
– Capital Gains Tax		(9)	(138)	(270)	(406)
Net Proceeds After-tax		1,726	1,932	2,166	2,430
Total return in Year of Sale		1,904	2,120	2,363	2,637

Annual After-tax Cash Flows with Sale at Year-end

		1	2	3	4
Equity	0	(2,015)	(2,015)	(2,015)	(2,015)
	1	1,904	179	179	179
After-tax	2		2,120	188	188
	3			2,363	198
Cash Flow	4				2,637
	5				
by Year	6				
	7				
	8				
	9				
	10				

		1	2	3	4
Internal Rate of Return		– 5.49%	7.11	11.54%	13.71%

Return on Current Estimated Value:

	1	2	3	4
After-tax Equity Value	1,726	1,932	2,166	2,430
Current After tax Cash Flow	179	188	198	207
Return on Current Equity Value	10.36%	9.75%	9.13%	8.52%

$\frac{5}{216}$	$\frac{6}{111}$	$\frac{7}{124}$	$\frac{8}{136}$	$\frac{9}{147}$	$\frac{10}{157}$
3,273	3,751	4,274	4,847	5,475	6,163
(545)	(660)	(782)	(911)	(1,047)	(1,191)
2,728	3,091	3,492	3,936	4,427	4,972
2,944	3,202	3,616	4,071	4,574	5,129

(2,015)	(2,015)	(2,015)	(2,015)	(2,015)	(2,015)
179	179	179	179	179	179
188	188	188	188	188	188
198	198	198	198	198	198
207	207	207	207	207	207
2,944	216	216	216	216	216
	3,202	111	111	111	111
		3,616	124	124	124
			4,071	136	136
				4,574	147
					5,129

14.93%	15.26%	15.46%	15.58%	15.63%	15.65%

2,728	3,091	3,492	3,936	4,427	4,972
216	111	124	136	147	157

7.91%	3.60%	3.54%	3.45%	3.32%	3.16%

What does all this mean? Perhaps another graph will help put it all in perspective. *Figure 2* charts four measures of return: The cash flow before and after-tax, shown as CFBT and CFAT, respectively; the IRR; and the percentage Return on Current Equity. Note that the annual return measures drop sharply in the sixth year because of our assumption that capital expenditures for leasing and tenant improvements would begin in the sixth year. We could have smoothed their effect, but it is interesting to see how differently they affect each.

Obviously, a number of key trends are underway, and an important point exists between the fifth and sixth years. Probably, the most important trend is the decline in the Return on Current Equity Value. After the fifth year, its growth rate begins to fall behind those of all the other measures, which are all computed using the initial equity investment.

In this example, the IRR is not as obvious an indicator as it could be. If the graph went a few more years, or if this property qualified for accelerated depreciation, you would see the IRR rise quickly, peak, and then drift steadily lower the longer the property is held. A reduction in the tax benefits over time compared to the increase in the Current Equity Value causes the downward drift.

In summary, almost all property investments reach such a "peak" return point, given the assumption that the preceding appreciation rate is fairly steady. Generally, the "optimum" period of ownership can be determined using the IRR and other measures. It is an unfortunate, and somewhat perverse, aspect of the tax laws that the longer you own a property, the lower your return becomes. Peak returns are mostly by-products of the tax laws.

While this pattern means that you can gauge your maximum dollar return for a given property, it does not guarantee other suitable investments will arise when you sell.

The assumptions of a steady appreciation, and stable capitalization rates are obviously important. If you create a financial forecast for your property similar in form to our example, you can also include both your current actual results, and your current knowledge about the key future assumptions. This information could give you a competitive edge when thinking about When to Sell.

A final point: We did not chart either net income or cash flow against book equity. While they may be meaningful to public companies with public reporting requirements, they are extremely misleading about the operations and prospects of a property. Many companies, particularly insurance companies, keep properties that yield high returns on a book basis but which would be an embarrassment if viewed on a current equity value yield.

Figure 2

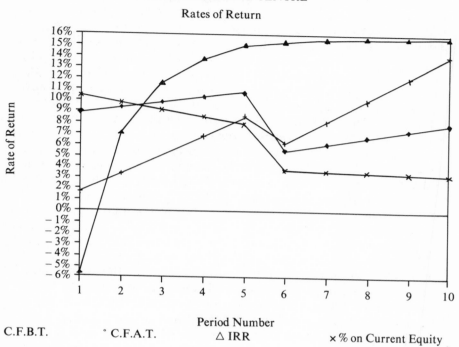

THE COMMERCIAL CENTRE
Rates of Return

C.F.B.T. ° C.F.A.T. △ IRR × % on Current Equity

HOW TO SELL

Selling is often harder than buying. When someone has been close to a project for a number of years, they often form emotional attachments to the investment. Sometimes, they also lose sight of the overall market after being deeply involved in the details.

Other reasons may make selling hard, as discussed earlier. The property is a known quality. Unless you are going to invest in insured, tax-free municipals, you are going to have to buy some new investment you know less about than the one you sold. Also, selling usually creates a tax liability that people sometimes try to avoid or defer with an irrational passion.

We wish to make three main points about selling: one is organizational, the other two are strategic. First, selling is done best when the responsibility and authority to sell is clearly defined, and if possible, is delegated to someone directly in the real estate business. Secondly, one must know the market. Finally, target the market.

Who Decides To Sell

Usually, real estate developers make the best sellers. They handle the responsibility of buying and selling constantly. They are experienced in the product and the ways it can be sold, know what they need, and look at selling as part of a continuing cycle of acquiring, creating value, and selling. They also know that sometimes it is better to make a deal than to get every last dollar of price.

Large corporations are often more adept at buying than selling. These sellers generally do not leave the sales decision to one or two key people. They require a committee of senior management and/or board members to pass on all but the most insignificant sale. We have worked with several multi-billion dollar companies that required all sales over $10,000 be approved by a board-level committee.

Sometimes, the time consumed by a large corporation in achieving consensus for a sale causes buyers to lose interest. Other times, this lengthy process works to the buyer's advantage.

For example, about four years ago, a San Francisco lithograph company was moving out of its large plant south of Market Street. The company's board did not want to throw the property open to bid. They decided to set a price, solicit bids from a small list of large, qualified developers, and negotiate a sale. The board hired a very reputable appraiser known to their home office in the midwest, who set the purchase price at 8 million dollars.

One developer offered one-half million dollars more than the asking price. In exchange, the seller would have to provide attractive financing (10%). The developer was awarded the negotiation rights, and after a couple of months, had a binding contract. He then found a financial partner and quickly closed the deal with the company.

Several new details emerged. It soon became apparent that the partners could not work well with each other. The financial partner agreed to buy out the developer. As this drawn-out negotiation was proceeding, a great deal of developer and investor interest built up in office bulding properties "South of Market." The buy-out consequently netted the developer a couple of million dollars for his half interest after less than a year. The financial partner also came out ahead because his cost was still well below market value.

In this scenario, we cannot say simply that the appraiser was wrong, because his value was rendered at a given point in time, However, the company probably should not have used an appraiser from outside the area who was unfamiliar with local trends. Also, the board should have let the market determine the price. If they wanted a quick sale, they should have sold for cash at a "wholesale" price. If they wanted retail, they should have marketed the property over a longer period without restricting the bid list. Their rigid criteria cost them millions of dollars.

We have all seen or heard about examples like this. It is called "buying right." It could just as well be called "selling wrong."

Whether in a large corporation or a small partnership, the politics involved in committing to a time, price, and terms often cause management to lose sight of what they are selling, or of how conditions are changing as they are selling. Often, management then makes the tacit decision not to sell, or they sell at yesterday's price.

Another interesting example of sellers who are "too tough to sell," is found in many of the railroad companies, public utilities, and quasi-municipal agencies. For the railroads who have owned their property ever since they pioneered rail lines across the U.S., real estate development is mostly an after-thought, or at best, a side-line to the operating companies. The real estate departments, if there are such separate entities, are not charged with creating a return on value, but with pre-serving and obtaining a return on assets held at an unrealistic, antiquated cost.

We have reviewed several proposals which involve building on land leased from railroads. In virtually every case, these leases were uneconomic except under perfect conditions. The railroads wanted an unsubordinated lease, a current market rent, open-ended rent increases every few years based on land fair market value without regard to current use, participation in overages, and extensive design approvals to name a few items. As a result of this tough stance, they discourage development that could give them a good return on value and generate income for their primary businesses.

There is often an "institutional" bias against active development. It seems that it is worse for an employee to make twenty good deals and one bad one, than to make three or four safe ones.

The solution to these problems is to set a clear policy of the goals and objectives for the company's real estate assets, with reasonable delegation of the decision-making authority. Assets should be fairly valued, and the departments should have to make a return on that value.

Know Your Product

Previously we developed a cash flow for a hypothetical commercial office building. By building such a model yourself, or having your accountant or other consultant build one, you will have information that is very useful. This is used not just to compute your tax liability, or your return if you were to sell. What is really important is to gather all the information together so that you, or someone who assists you, can analyze the figures and compare them with similar properties.

Most syndication buyers create their own models of how a property is expected to operate over a 5-to-10-year period. They base their figures on current operating numbers, comparable properties, and their own judgement of how they could improve operations. These buyers will often use these figures as arguments for concessions from the seller, because the forecasted return is too low. If you have your own set of figures, you should be able to evaluate the validity of their argument. Do they have a legitimate point, or are they just negotiating?

Comparisons with other similar properties yields extremely important facts. Has your property been operated as efficiently as the competition? It is of little gain to negotiate a sale at an eight percent cap rate in a nine percent cap rate market when your expenses are 10% higher, and your income 10% lower, than everyone else's. The buyer may be counting on improving the net income just by effective property management, and end up with a real cap rate over 10%.

For investors who are not in the real estate business full-time, we usually recommend that they commission an appraisal. We do not recommend the appraisal for the value opinion because appraised values are limited to a point in time without regard to the tax-oriented type of sales that drive much of the market. But, the appraisals contain good information about the property's physical condition, the competitive market rents, competitive operating expenses, and cap rates of recent sales.

Using this document as a source, the seller then needs to poll a number of real estate brokers about their opinion of the property's value, and the market in general. The seller should also ask them for references from recent clients.

Personally, I have usually found it better to work a sale through brokers rather than avoiding them. Buyers often have their own broker anyway, so why let them get all the fee for representing the buyer? Sellers who refuse to pay for any brokerage commission also refuse to recognize that if the buyer is paying one of his own, he is paying you less than he would if he had not employed one.

Also, as we said in the beginning, real estate is not very liquid. The marketing period for a property, depending on how aggressive a price you're asking, is from a couple of months to over half a year or longer. When you have decided to sell a property, a holding cost is implied for continuing to carry the property. If a broker is capable of shortening the period of sale by a few months because he has contacts with a wide number of buyers, he has earned his fee.

So, you now should have the information to make an informed judgment on what to ask for the property. You should also know who you may want to market it.

Before continuing, we would like to give an example of the importance of knowing your product. In the mid-1970s, I negotiated two joint ventures with an investor from Beverly Hills whose philosophy was to buy under-managed properties. He and his staff would make over 100 purchase offers per year, sight unseen, on all types of older income properties. The offers were laced with all sorts of contingencies that allowed them to inspect and analyze the property before putting any money at risk.

Most offers were rejected outright. However, a significant number — around 15 or 20 — were countered. From these, they focused on whether or not the income and operating costs were comparable to the market, and the soundness of the structures. Because significant deferred maintenance was usually needed, they negotiated some provision for price reduction or carry-back financing to cover the cost.

At the end of a year, they had bought only one or two properties. They knew though that within one year, they could increase the net income, and value, by 15 to 25% just by curing deferred maintenance problems, aggressive leasing, and vacancy control.

In these situations, the sellers were not little old ladies who did not know any better. Our first purchase was a 400 unit apartment project from a major public syndicator, one of the top 10 today. The second was from a smaller partnership. After I had left that company, they formed a third joint venture and purchased a large commercial complex from its original developer. In each case, the owners had undervalued their assets.

Target Your Market

The final point is to target your market — based upon the type of property you have, and the buyers who are active in the market. This will determine to whom you should sell.

A very knowledgeable investment broker we know maintains that the commercial brokerage business today is much different than even *five years ago*. It used to be that the key to making a sale was introducing the right people to the right setting. Financial figures were of the most simple construction, and contracts were more straight forward. Today, that portion of the buying market still exists, but it commands a much smaller proportion of the activity.

In the broadest sense, three major capital markets may be tapped for investment real estate: the private investor, the syndicator, and the institutional markets.

If the institutional market is not the biggest, it is certainly the fastest growing one. The entry of pension funds with their megabillion assets into the real estate investment market has been felt in every location in the U.S. Because they are neither concerned with income taxation, nor with leverage, and are substantially freed from stifling investment regulations at a time when their assets are growing faster than the U.S. economy as a whole, these players have revolutionized the ownership structure of real estate.

When a single pension fund decides to adjust its portfolio from 8 percent of its assets in real estate to 10 percent, several extra million dollars are suddenly looking for products to buy. When the whole industry decides to do the same thing, we are talking about billions of dollars, every year! Best of all, they make all-cash purchases.

This effect has not been without some less desirable consequences. In a recent conference hosted by the Bay Area Real Estate Research Council, a representative of a major private development firm pointed out that it was becoming far more difficult to build economic office building projects. The institutions were building and buying property almost without regard for current market conditions.

For example, Denver, nicknamed the "See-Through City" because of substantially empty office buildings, had a glut of office space; yet, new buildings were still being built. Across the country, similar over-building trends have been fueled largely by institutional demand motivated mainly by portfolio considerations, not investment criteria. Of course, this trend can be good for sellers, if the market is not already so overbuilt that it depresses value.

The second major capital market force is the syndications. These buyers are primarily motivated by tax considerations, and to a much lesser extent, capital appreciation. As buyers, syndications require purchase contracts that allow special allocations of the purchase price, and deferred payments of a portion of that price. Without good tax and legal advice, a seller may find that the effect of these structures may be less advantageous than a discounted, all-cash sale.

Finally, there is the private investment market. This market is largely restricted to well-leveraged properties valued under $10,000,000. Motivations, for this class of investors, are as varied as people themselves.

So, how do you target your property to these capital markets? First, you need to know about the potential buyers' goals.

Pension funds seek capital preservation, income, and inflation protection, in that order. They do not want residential property. This leaves them with commercial, income producing property such as office buildings, shopping centers, unsubordinated land leases, and master-leased hotels and warehouses where the credit on the lease is triple-A rated. They also want the best locations and exellent quality construction.

Syndications want to maximize the tax benefits to their investors, and minimize the possibility of negative cash flows that would have to be funded by the general partners. Apartments have become the preferred investment vehicle because of the generous depreciation allowances, and rents that are not subject to long-term leases. They will pay for good locations.

Private investors have motives that include some of the above, but they are often motivated by intangibles such as "pride of ownership." Other investors deal in "junk" property because the current returns are better, and it is cheaper because it's in disrepair or in a poor neighborhood.

Given these general classes of buyers, where does your property fit best? While this does not mean that you should only target that

JAMES MADDEN

market, it does give you a reference on judging the likelihood and sincerity of a buyer who does not fit the profile.

Merchandising

We have found it beneficial to prepare a package of information suited for each market type. Actually, you should prepare one package that includes general information such as a few professional quality photographs, the legal description, location and plat map, floor plans, historical operating results, and a current rent roll. To this package, you should add, where appropriate, financing information, the forecast for next year's operating results, and any information that may be of particular interest to a particular buyer. For instance, for an institutional package, you would stress the number of national firms that are tenants, proportion of tenants with high credit ratings, other prestige buildings or companies located nearby, and the quality of the improvements or maintenance. For the syndicator, you would stress the number of tenants whose leases are below market rents, and when their leases expire.

Finally, whether you are using a broker or not, you need to make it known that your property is for sale. Good signage and advertisements in high circulation papers are a must. A listing on a multiple listing service (MLS) is also very effective.

Direct mailings to pension funds, insurance companies, syndicators and private investors probably will not be as effective if you have not already qualified their interest by phone. Institutions, in particular, hesitate to work on purchasing a property that is being "shotgunned" all over town. Part of that hesitancy centers on the amount of paperwork (written reports, appraisals, proformas and cash flows) that their investment decisions require. If you can deliver a package that has a lot of this work done already, you can probably shop it around to more than one or two major buyers at the same time.

All of this preparation requires a lot of work, but it will be much easier if you keep your records up to date on a regular basis. Remember, you never know when you may decide that you want to, or need to sell. Be prepared. Then, you only have to assemble your research and evaluate the offers you receive.

CONCLUSION

We have covered a lot of territory in this chapter. First, we pointed out that as an owner, you have many rights to sell, and many alternatives in lieu of an outright sale.

Next we discussed reasons why you might wish to sell. The principal reason will always be to satisfy your own goals. Selling is not con-trolled strictly by quantitive measures such as money or rates of return. Personal factors — ego, pride, convenience, personal resources, personal tax position, and the choice among available investment alternatives — are central to the sales decision.

How to sell was discussed in three parts: Who makes the decision? Evaluate what you have. Target your market.

The key point is that selling has to be viewed from *your own perspective*. You need to set forth explicit goals, and decide how your property can meet these goals. Then, the decision, *When to Sell*, becomes a process to a new beginning.

James Madden is president of James S. Madden & Company, which is located in San Francisco. Mr. Madden's company provides real estate investment advisory services to individuals and pension funds. In addition, the firm is currently providing project management services for the rehabilitation and syndication of a 50-year-old office building in Southern California.